SHELL SHOCKED

SHELL SHOCKED

HOW CANADIANS CAN INVEST AFTER THE COLLAPSE

JOHN STEPHENSON

John Wiley & Sons Canada, Ltd.

Library and Archives Canada Cataloguing in Publication Data

Stephenson, John, 1962-
   Shell shocked : how Canadians can invest after the collapse /
John Stephenson.

Includes index.
ISBN 978-0-470-16087-9

   1. Investments—Canada. 2. Finance, Personal—Canada. I. Title.
HG4521.S7567 2009   332.6'0971   C2009-902927-8

Production Credits
Cover and Interior Design: Adrian So
Typesetter: Thomson
Printer: Tri-Graphic Printing

John Wiley & Sons Canada, Ltd.
6045 Freemont Blvd.
Mississauga, Ontario
L5R 4J3

Printed in Canada

1 2 3 4 5 TRI 13 12 11 10 09

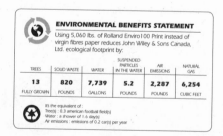

ENVIRONMENTAL BENEFITS STATEMENT
Using 5,060 lbs. of Rolland Enviro100 Print instead of virgin fibres paper reduces John Wiley & Sons Canada, Ltd. ecological footprint by:

TREES	SOLID WASTE	WATER	SUSPENDED PARTICLES IN THE WATER	AIR EMISSIONS	NATURAL GAS
13 FULLY GROWN	820 POUNDS	7,739 GALLONS	5.2 POUNDS	2,287 POUNDS	6,254 CUBIC FEET

It's the equivalent of :
Tree(s) : 0.3 american football field(s)
Water : a shower of 1.6 day(s)
Air emissions : emissions of 0.2 car(s) per year

TABLE OF CONTENTS

PREFACE

It was a daunting task. I had to find $100 million in additional earnings by the end of the quarter—only three weeks away—so the company could make its numbers. But how? I was only two years out of MBA school. What could I possibly contribute to Enron Corporation's financial success? My answer arrived in the form of a cardboard box stuffed full of energy contracts for natural gas delivery stretching many years into the future. Within those contracts lay the answer to Enron's $100-million shortfall. They were to be mined for money, money that Enron would use to demonstrate that it had once again met Wall Street analysts' earnings expectations for yet another quarter. Actually, the real trick was to beat analysts' consensus expectations by a penny a share.

It was the summer of 1996, and I was determined to make a go of my new role as a manager for Enron in Houston, Texas. But I had trouble shaking the feeling that something about Enron wasn't quite right. Years later, in 2001, my suspicions were confirmed when the company's stock price hurtled toward zero over revelations that, hiding off the company's balance sheet, were enormous liabilities. At the time it came down, the Enron bankruptcy was the largest in U.S. history.

In the summer of 2008, I watched stocks tumble once again. This time around, I was working as a portfolio manager for First Asset Funds Inc. in Toronto. But it wasn't just a few stocks going down: it was pretty well every stock on every exchange. Then it dawned on me what was happening—Wall Street had mimicked Enron and had put the entire market on steroids. The large Wall Street investment banks had been juicing their earnings with profits from risky trading and unrealistic assumptions. Worse yet, they had enhanced their earnings by employing tremendous amounts of leverage. In the process, the American financial services sector had gone to 23 per cent of total market capitalization in 2007 from just 6 per cent of market capitalization in 1980. Even more remarkable, this industry had grown to represent a staggering 40 per cent of *total* corporate profits in America.

But much of that growth was based on faulty logic, bluster and bravado. And when news got out that behind these impressive sales and earnings reports was simply a lot of hot air, the market began to exact a painful retribution on U.S. and global banks. Share prices tumbled quickly, with the banks that traded and originated the most toxic paper—the stuff linked to subprime mortgages in the U.S.—falling hardest. It wasn't just U.S. banks that had drunk the Kool-Aid, however, it was the European banks, too; in a desperate bid to achieve massive scale, they had leveraged themselves up as much as sixty to one. In other words, they had used fifty-nine dollars of borrowed money for each dollar of their own.

With banks going bust, governments around the world sprang into action. "Bailout!" became the rallying cry of industries looking for liquidity injections. Everyone was looking for help from government. Amidst all the mayhem, Canada, while not exactly lily-white in the whole affair, nevertheless found itself standing apart from the crowd—in a *good* way. Somehow, we were spared the worst of the carnage.

And then it hit me. It was all so obvious. Canada was going to emerge just fine from the fast lane to ruin. More than fine, actually. We were going to be light years ahead of the competition, which would be digging its way out of holes for decades. As well, in an ironic twist, it was going to be our boring old resources that were going to help us navigate the way forward.

I also realized that, probably more than any other financial expert out there, I could explain to Canadian investors what the linkages were and how the pieces fit together. Why? Because I was *there*. All the pieces of my eclectic background suddenly coalesced, putting me in a unique position to see beyond the headlines and make sense of what, for most people, was simply economic Armageddon. I also became aware of another truth: that Canada and Asia are on the rise, albeit for very different reasons. Nonetheless, our futures have become irrevocably intertwined.

The global financial crisis that started in America has now enveloped the entire world. I find it interesting, though, that the Chinese symbol for crisis actually comprises two symbols: one means danger, but the other means opportunity. How appropriate. The times may be uncertain, but they are offering us a once-in-a-generation opportunity for investment riches. This book is for people who still have a little of their savings left; those who know they need to do *something* and realize that hope is not a practical solution for an approaching retirement. The key to successful investing is to anticipate change, particularly monumental change, and to act before the herd. This book is your road map to those changes.

The world is indeed transforming, and dramatically so. Old, familiar players on the world stage, like the United States, will play supporting roles in the future. China, on the other hand, will be playing the lead, while Canada, the only other nation to come through this mess largely unfettered, will be the new world's rising star. Why? Simply put, we have what the rest of the world needs and they will come to us to get it.

Shell Shocked examines where the world has been, what that future is expected to hold and what investors should do about it. Is this the perfect plan? Of course not! But it is an excellent blueprint, and armed with a blueprint of what to look for, investors can position themselves well for the future. Investing, like many other things in life, is a lifestyle choice. This book isn't about timing the market; it's about understanding the way the world works, a world where commodities, gold, residential housing, agriculture, banks, utilities, food retailers, brokerages, high technology firms, industrial companies and insurance firms all play a role. What makes the stocks of some companies go up while others go down? It's about great companies and not-so-great companies. But mostly, it's about Canada rising on the world stage and how you can invest profitably in the opportunities ahead.

1

CANADA RISING

Canada gets no respect! For as long as I can remember, we've thought of our home and native land as a sleepy branch plant economy. Anyone with any ambition had to head south of the border to make a fortune. Canada was just too small, too conservative and too unproductive an economy to play with the big boys. Yes, the United States was *it* and we, as Canadians, had to just thank our lucky stars that we happened to live right beside such a big, successful and generous neighbour.

But Canada is rising. Everything you've heard about Canada's supposed mediocrity is about to be proved wrong. All of the things the naysayers have said are *exactly why* this is the country best positioned to survive the collapse of the Western world's financial system. Too conservative? Too risk averse? Our cautious nature helped keep our chartered banks out of major trouble when the world was lapping up the toxic securities that American investment bankers were out there peddling. Too weak on productivity? While our national productivity has been nothing to write home about, at least it wasn't based on a lie—like in America. No global brands? Just you wait. Research In Motion is on the move and so, too, is Royal Bank of Canada, which is picking up the star employees of disgraced Wall Street giants. Our lack of entrepreneurial drive is another shortcoming the pundits like to hurl our way. Maybe, but that dog-eat-dog type of entrepreneurial zing that is so much a part of American life was the Achilles heel of its investment banking industry. Best of all, Canada's focus on natural resources is exactly what will be needed when the dust clears on the collapse and the startling truth becomes plain: economic power has shifted away from the United States to the emerging markets in Asia.

Despite all this, investors are petrified. They have seen their wealth destroyed and their prospects dim in a global financial tsunami. We have witnessed the greatest financial cataclysm of our lifetimes. We don't know how this train wreck will end, but we are certain of one thing—it will end badly. At the heart of this disaster was a very simple supposition that turned out to be tragically flawed. Upon that flawed supposition, financial products were designed, lies were told and whole industries were created. When the lies and promises were finally exposed for the hot air that they really were, the punishment meted out was devastating. Globally, trillions of dollars have been eviscerated in one dramatic wave of selling after another. Stocks, bonds, commodities, currencies, real estate, you name it and it's gone up in smoke. Years of work, good intentions and dreams have all been lost in the ether. No wonder investors are shell shocked and scared to death.

To invest, you need to trust. You need to trust that the system is fair. You need to trust that there is at least a reasonable expectation of earning a decent return for all of your troubles.

Yet, all of the experts misled you. They failed to warn you of the land mines that were planted on the road to investment riches. Instead, they fed into your greed and told you what you wanted to hear, rather than what you *needed* to hear. For the most part, these experts were employed by the very same people who were the architects of this disaster—the Wall Street wizards. These wizards lied to you, they lied to their clients and they lied to one another. It was a very big lie and a very convincing lie, but once the market figured out that there was something rotten in the state of Denmark, the jig was up.

In punishing session after punishing session, markets around the globe have created the most massive fire sale the world has ever seen, sending valuations crashing to multi-decade lows. In less than three months, stock exchanges around the world shed more than $34 trillion—the largest and quickest loss of stock market wealth ever.

Plunging stock values are one thing, but what's keeping us up at night is not just our declining net worth—it's the impact this financial crisis might be having on the *real* economy. We've always heard that when America catches a cold, Canada gets the flu. Is it really going to be any different this time? In America unemployment is up, consumer confidence is down and the auto industry is almost sure to collapse, leading us to wonder if Canada can be far behind.

Yet, Canada is doing just fine. While it is only natural to be cautious, there's no reason to be paralyzed by uncertainty. On just about every measure, Canada is ahead of the pack. We have the best fiscal situation of any G8 country. Our banking system, while not unblemished, has survived the meltdown and is in an ideal position to cherry-pick the cream of the crop globally. Canada's housing sector, while over-valued, never saw the excesses so prevalent in the United Kingdom and the United States. We have a national health care system, our government sector is strong and our reputation globally has been enhanced rather than diminished with this ordeal. And, in the emerging world order, Asia will be ascending and America will be falling. A rapidly industrializing Asia will be hungry for all things Canadian. Our much maligned resource sector will be front and centre in this rising wave of prosperity led not by America but by Asia.

The biggest casualty of all has been the American mystique, which has been shattered. The United States, as the largest, most successful economy, was until recently the envy of the world and the safe haven in times of trouble. Nothing symbolized American power and success more than the Wall Street banks and the masters of the universe who inhabited them. But after the collapse, a truth became clear. Like America's citizens, these financial institutions were living well beyond their means. Their collective credit cards were maxed out and when problems started to appear, the banks fell fast and hard. The speed at which the long-established banking system unravelled caught even the most seasoned investors by surprise.

No longer is the United States the undisputed leader in all things global, as a perfect storm of its own making has destroyed its biggest and most revered corporations. Neither the U.S. mystique, nor its economy, will soon be back.

I, too, sought my fortune in the U.S. As a young man, I decided there was a wide-open world out there and I wanted a part of it. So after finishing my engineering degree at the University of Waterloo, I headed for France to study—of all things—business. Armed with an MBA from the Institut Européen d'Administration des Affaires (INSEAD), I truly believed the world was indeed global and, quite possibly, my oyster. And no country had a more commanding global footprint than the United States of America. I bought the company line that the U.S. really did have the better model. So I voted with my feet. I moved to the United States.

I aimed straight for New York, but somehow landed in Houston. At least my job was with a good company that was really going places. Enron, after all, was starting to make waves for its success in turning a sleepy pipeline company into a global energy marketing and trading company. It was going to be the world's first natural gas *major*, or so the banner in the lobby proclaimed.

It wasn't long before the corporate accolades were pouring in. Enron was voted the most innovative company by *Fortune* magazine year after year and it was climbing up the ranks, becoming one of America's most admired corporations. Stock analysts loved the company as well. But what I and my friends in Enron's pool of associates and analysts couldn't understand was how the company made *any* money. All around us seemed to be failed projects and busted deals.

Enron fabricated earnings to keep its share price high—Wall Street posted impressive results, too, until it didn't. To think that I had a ringside seat to watch the two most fascinating and sickening financial disasters of recent memory, all within a span of seven years! The motivations were the same—massive short-term rewards for the insiders, with no regard for the longer-term consequences of their actions. Talented people, who could have made a valuable contribution to society as doctors or architects, were seduced into careers in finance and into the clutches of Enron by a culture of easy money and instant gratification.

Wall Street was no different from Enron. In fact, it was a whole lot worse. It, too, seduced smart people with the prospect of unfathomable riches and used its talents to further the goals of the top brass. And, like Enron, Wall Street moved away from its traditional lines of business toward the more arcane and exotic, while all the time proclaiming *We're creating shareholder value.*

In retrospect, I wonder how anyone could have believed at all in that era. It was all about broadband trading and the Internet craze. We even invented newfangled metrics like "eyeballs" and "clicks" to justify valuations rather than the traditional earnings and cash flow metrics that stock analysts pore over. The Internet, the valuations the tech stocks commanded and the investor carnage in the aftermath were a product of slick Wall Street marketing and spin, the same forces that would unleash themselves on the world stage with far greater effect in 2008.

So I headed for home. My dream of a Wall Street career in tatters, I left the big leagues and started over. I wasn't going to London or even Chicago. I was going home to Toronto, hardly a global financial capital.

I started over, as a portfolio manager, for First Asset Funds, a midsized Canadian mutual fund company where I specialized in resource and infrastructure investing. Covering Canadian equities, I quickly learned what separated Canada from the rest of the pack. Our companies aren't all that flashy, but for the most part what they produce are *real* things—things like dishwashers, cars and subways. Things people need. I learned about the stock market. I toured our mines and oil sands projects. When I was done, I was convinced that Canada has what the world needs. So I resolved to learn all that I could and to put together a blueprint for the future jammed full of practical investment advice that I and others could follow. I needed to move fast, because the world was changing quickly. New countries were on the rise and others were falling and in the process altering the investment landscape.

Something magical began to happen: after years of economic isolation, on December 11, 2001, China was granted membership in the World Trade Organization. All of a sudden, China was part of the club. And with its voracious appetite for energy and materials, it showed its potential to transform the Canadian economy.

China's rise is unstoppable. But it isn't just China that is on the move; India and Southeast Asia are also going places and dragging Canada along for the ride. While many fret that China will be hobbled as America retrenches, the truth is that America needs China—not the other way around. China has the money, it has the people and it has the political will to keep on growing, *regardless* of what is happening in America.

In 2007, I was in China on business. I was flabbergasted by what I saw. Everywhere, people were on the move, with a determination and vitality you rarely see at home. Emerging out of former fields were whole cityscapes, but not just ordinary buildings; these were modern architectural masterpieces proclaiming *We have arrived*. But it is the people, the hundreds of millions of people yearning for a better life, who are the force behind China's remarkable transformation—a stunning transformation that has occurred in just thirty years.

What America did over the last century, China is doing as well—only faster. Behind the miracle is a culture that reveres education, hard work and savings, the very things America used to value but somehow forgot in the rush toward instant gratification. A Chinese-born colleague, Erik Yan, told me how lucky he feels to have his education behind him and to be living in Canada. He told me about his niece, who studied seven days a week from seven in the morning to midnight for the chance to attend a better *high school*. That's how intense the competition is in China. It's also one reason China's rise is simply unstoppable—because her people are.

Average working people in China and India save 35 per cent of their income. In North America, we save almost nothing. While the situation isn't great in Canada, it's worse in the U.S., where Americans spend more than they make. To fund this rampant consumption, Americans need to borrow and borrow big. And when Uncle Sam needs money to balance his chequebook, it is the Chinese and others with their excess savings who are willing to lend him the money.

The slightly more than a billion people in the West have most of the world's creature comforts, but very little savings. The rest of the world has more than five billion people—a number that is growing fast—and they want what we have. They are willing to work a whole lot harder, and for a whole lot less. Unless you really think that everyone in China is going back to riding on bicycles, you have to be excited about the companies that supply the *real things* that China and the rest of the developing world need.

Canada, on the other hand, is in good shape. Alone among the major economies of the West, ours has come through the terrible collapse with its health reasonably intact. We are selling more abroad than we import. Unlike America, where the U.S. government has spent trillions of dollars to shore up its financial sector, our institutions are solid. Canadian taxpayers won't be saddled with massive public debts from one desperate bailout after another, as American taxpayers will.

Our companies are well positioned for the global economy of the future. The financial health of our leading firms is, for the most part, excellent. Our leading companies aren't saddled with unwieldy debts. They will be moving forward, while their U.S. competitors are digging out from under a mountain of debt. The crazy, overzealous risk-taking approach to American business has been disgraced globally. It will be a long time, if ever, before a German or Chinese portfolio manager will trust an American investment bank enough to buy its structured investment vehicle crammed full of questionable credits. Canada's unheralded financial sector will have uncontested access to the global playing field.

The oil sands in Alberta are an incredible resource. The scope and scale of the resource basin and industrial complex is staggering. The largest industrial complex in the world is in the Edmonton and Fort McMurray corridor. At Syncrude Canada's facility, the enormous deposits of sandy oil stretch for kilometres in every direction. The tires on the dump trucks that haul this resource from where it is mined to the upgrader units for further processing are enormous. While I stand more than six feet tall, I couldn't even reach the midpoint on one of the tires of these enormous machines. Without doubt, Canada, which sits atop the second-largest oil reserves in the world, is destined to be an energy superpower.

Descending more than two kilometres below the earth's surface, I arrived at a small underground city where they were mining for gold. I was visiting the LaRonde gold mine, owned by Canada's Agnico-Eagle Mines Limited in northern Quebec. Little did I know it, but the elevator shaft in which I descended had taken me to the deepest point in the Western hemisphere. Underground was a small city of trucks, men and machines—all in the pursuit of recovering gold. In an era when the U.S. dollar is so obviously a flawed currency, Canada, whose mining companies produce more than half the world's gold, will be well positioned to benefit in this new world of tomorrow.

Compared with past cycles in which resources boomed and then crashed, the rally in resources next time around will be sustained for much, much longer. Resource companies, unlike American investment banks, produce something tangible. With large swatches of the American investment landscape so tarnished, investors will be willing to pay a premium for companies that produce something where there are no substitutes, demand is voracious and supply is tight. Canada is well positioned to be the biggest beneficiary of the coming resources boom.

But Canada has more than resources. It has expertise, too. In smart phone design, Research In Motion of Waterloo, Ontario, is a global leader. In insurance, our national champions are stellar performers. Our expertise in mining, heavy oil and infrastructure development will be in great demand in the future.

That's great news for Canada and investors in Canadian stocks, regardless of where they might live. As the world digs itself out from economic calamity, Canada will emerge stronger than ever. And so let the battle cry sound: *Buy me all the Canada you can get!*

2
AMERICA FALLING

We've heard it countless times; it's even enshrined in the U.S. Declaration of Independence: America is a land of dreams, a land where anything is possible if you believe in yourself and are willing to work hard.

America's power, influence and status as the world's only superpower put it in a category all by itself. America is so central to the world as we know it that it is difficult to imagine it not always playing the starring role. As a young fortune seeker, I, like so many others before, was drawn to the possibilities offered by America's riches. I wanted a shot at the good life. For a while, I thought I had found it at a natural gas company that was suddenly on the move—Enron. As I was to learn first-hand, when you strip away the bricks and mortar of a business and take it in a new fast-track and highly innovative direction, you had better be damn sure the guys running the place are ethical.

The global financial collapse has drawn back the curtain on the United States, exposing it for what it has become—a hollowed-out Wal-Mart, with shoppers frantically searching for the next great deal. But the deals, or the next big thing, will be a long time coming. Just like

Enron, which deceived the world for a while with its fancy accounting chicanery, the U.S., though still strong, has fallen hard. While we would all like to cling to the image of what America was, the truth of what it has become is sobering. The subprime mortgage fiasco has turned Wall Street into a ghost town. National and personal debts are at all-time highs. U.S. consumers have lost trillions in their pension funds and stock holdings, and real estate, the so-called best investment you could ever make, has been trashed in the wake of this disaster. Greed, lack of regulatory oversight and a short-term winner-take-all type of high-stakes Vegas casino Texas Hold'em mentality was at the core of this disaster. Wall Street, government officials and silly and stupid home-buyers were all to blame. But the death of Wall Street is prologue. This disaster is so large, so consequential, that America will never have the same moral and economic authority that it has enjoyed for the last fifty years. Never.

America will always be a serious competitor, but it has been badly winded and beaten. The blow that crippled America came from within. America is down on the mat and it will eventually recover. It just won't be getting off the mat anytime soon.

GO BIG OR GO HOME

The American Dream drew us all in: the chance to own a home, to own a business, to make it big has inspired millions to make the journey to America's shores. Would-be entrepreneurs have been willing to risk it all for a chance at the good life in the United States, a country that represents the be-all and end-all of free market capitalism. Its large population, uniform language and business-friendly culture have allowed the U.S. to grow prosperous and to spawn businesses ranging from small start-ups to huge multinational corporations. Boeing, General Electric, Microsoft and Coca-Cola are just a few of the American brands that are known and admired the world over.

By the numbers, America is an impressive place. Its economy is the largest in the world, accounting for about $14 trillion, or 25.5 per cent, of global economic activity. With a population of more than 300 million people, it has the third-largest population in the world, ranking solidly behind two behemoths, China and India. America's large population and its culture, which is focused on instant gratification, have made it a shopper's paradise. You can get whatever you like, however you like, whenever you like.

By extension, America is also the ultimate market for retailers. Consumption in the U.S. is totally stunning by any yardstick, with the American consumer accounting for 18 per cent of the world's economic activity and 72 per cent of America's gross domestic product. The square footage of retail space in the U.S. on a per capita basis is twice that of Canada's.

The enormous size of the American economy, its low personal tax rates and the limited government involvement in its economy have created an extremely competitive business climate. Winning in America means winning big, because of the sheer size of the market and a consuming public market that is predisposed to say yes to service offerings. With such a large market and so much potential, Americans and American business work hard.

The dominance of its economy is only part of the reason America has become such a force in the world; the other is its military might. The U.S. annually spends in excess of $710 billion, or 48.4 per cent of global military spending, to maintain its armed services. Even more astounding is the fact that America spends as much on its military as do the next thirty-five countries combined.

But America leads in ways besides its economic and military power. It is through its ideals—democracy, personal freedom and capitalism— that the U.S. has the greatest impact. And, more than any other nation, the U.S. has been willing to act to provide global leadership in support of its ideals.

ENRON: A HARBINGER OF WHAT WAS TO COME

I had just returned home, a newly minted MBA from INSEAD, eager to get working and out of my parents' house, when I received an unexpected phone call. It was Greg Wolfe calling from Enron Corporation in Houston, Texas, to see "if ya'll'd like an interview." Of course I would, but first I needed to figure out exactly what it was that Enron did. I put Greg off until the next day so I could do a little research.

The possibility of what Enron could become first occurred to a smart young management consultant named Jeffrey Skilling. While at McKinsey and Company, the world's leading strategy consultancy, Skilling realized that deregulation of the natural gas industry could be the opportunity to launch Enron into the big leagues. He pitched the concept to Ken Lay, Enron's chief executive officer, who could also see the possibilities. It wasn't long before Skilling was an Enron employee and the company began its rapid transformation from sleepy pipeline operator to energy investment bank.

In 1987, the world of natural gas changed as the U.S. Federal Energy Regulatory Commission began the process of deregulating the natural gas business. It seemed like a great idea at the time: customers could choose when they got their natural gas, in what quantity and from which supplier. But behind that very simple idea lay a world of possibilities for any company enterprising enough to jump into the confusion that existed in the marketplace. Enron, with Skilling and Lay at the helm, was just the kind of company to see the massive opportunity this change created and become filthy rich in the process.

It wouldn't occur to me until much later, but deregulation in the natural gas business perfectly paralleled what was to happen later on Wall Street—namely, that loose regulation created tremendous short-term opportunities for those at the top. But by giving the inmates the keys to the asylum and by transferring the ultimate risk of corporate bankruptcy to the shareholders, you gave a free pass to executives to make hay while the sun shone.

To change the world, you first need to change the employee base. No longer would pipeline guys cut it in the new Enron. Gone were the days when being a company man—a lifer—mattered. In the new world of Enron, the skills needed were the same as those that mattered on Wall Street: financing and trading skills. To get those skills, Enron went on a hiring binge, lapping up talent from the best business schools. But it wasn't just MBAs that Enron needed. It also needed "geeks"—PhDs in physics, economics and math—to create the kind of newfangled energy products that the company was going to sell. I was part of that new wave of hiring.

It was 1995 and Enron was on fire. We were taking the natural gas business and then the newly deregulating electricity business by storm. I was hired, along with hundreds of other MBAs and analysts, to help structure these new products. We structured gas contracts with imbedded options and financing streams. Heck, we even made markets for products such as newsprint right out of thin air.

As the market became more sophisticated, Enron's products became more complex. Bored with buying just regular ten-year gas contracts? No problem. Enron could design a ten-year gas contract that hedged your exposure to weather patterns and we'd even help take some of your liabilities off the balance sheet. All for a hefty fee, of course. As the company grew, so did its brain trust. Pretty soon Enron had more MBAs, lawyers and math geeks than you could shake a stick at—and they were all making tons of money.

But something strange was going on. My bosses would come to me and my colleagues and say we needed to find $100 million in extra profit before the end of the quarter. Sometimes, there would be only three or four weeks left in the quarter. How were we supposed to do it? We were given stacks of natural gas contracts that were for gas delivery all around the country, for years into the future. Our task, to help the company make the numbers, was to re-price these contracts. We changed the receipt point for gas delivery or made other assumptions that would boost our revenues or slash our costs. Then, we re-ran the models and made sure the auditors understood we were going to show a mark-to-market gain on the contracts. That way, we could book extra profits for the quarter, all with the use of a little financial engineering and some Excel keystrokes. It was all so simple. But was it ethical?

With more growth, plain vanilla gas deals were out and bandwidth trading was in. More complexity required more geeks and more dealmakers to stuff these new creations down the throats of financially illiterate utility companies throughout North America. With more and more products, plenty of traders were needed to trade around our positions or to exploit opportunities in a wide variety of commodity markets. If natural gas was cheap and power was dear, our traders could create a synthetic transaction where we bought gas and sold power. Some traders with only a few years on the job were pulling in seven-figure bonuses.

But the star employees were worth it. Enron, in a matter of ten short years, had transformed itself from a boring pipeline operation to one of America's "most-admired companies" and the seventh-largest corporation in the country. The key to Enron's success was simple: it showed Wall Street it could deliver consistently higher earnings, quarter after quarter, and was rewarded with a soaring share price.

The employees loved it. As Enron stock kept rising, many of them were becoming overnight millionaires. For the guys at the top, like Jeff Skilling and Ken Lay, the deal was even sweeter. Their annual compensation, when stock options were exercised, could easily top $10 million a year. Enron was blazing new trails and, for a while, everybody loved it—most of all the Wall Street wizards themselves.

But for me and many of my colleagues, this was a troubling time. None of us could understand how shuffling paperwork back and forth was creating any long-term shareholder value. We shared a broader concern: once you hollow out the core, the bricks and mortar of the business, and you replace it with financial engineering, isn't the corporate culture increasingly important? And Enron's corporate culture was rotten. It was all about short-term gains for the lucky few.

Enron's stock was ascending, but many of us weren't. If your group was on fire, then you were laughing. Money was rolling your way, stock options too. And other up-and-comers in the organization were looking to join your group. If not, you were looking for the next big opportunity to latch on to. While Enron was dynamic, it was also in perpetual crisis mode. All that mattered was making the quarter and pulling your numbers. There was no long-term planning. It was all short-term thinking and grabbing as much loot as you could while the getting was good. After three and a half years with Enron, another opportunity came my way. Ironically, it was to work as a management consultant to help other companies in the industry become more "Enron-like." If only they had known.

Then Enron stumbled. Earnings failed to meet expectations. *Why couldn't Enron release a balance sheet?* Wall Street analyst Richard Grubman demanded on an investor conference call. The finger pointing began and so, too, did management's stammering. This last quarter was just an aberration, they claimed. But then it wasn't. News began to surface that Enron was actually losing money in some of the crazy new businesses that, at first blush, had appeared so profitable. Its famous risk management practices no longer seemed to work. Incredibly, Enron's financial maestros had even used the value of their own stock to hedge an investment they made in another company. Could it really be true?

It *was* true. The geeks had got it wrong. The carefully designed hedges and offsetting transactions were really a mirage designed to cover up an inconvenient truth and Enron was a sitting duck. Despite all the bluster and bravado, the company was losing money in some of its core businesses. It had lied to Wall Street and the repercussions were immense. As news of losses and questionable business practices began to surface, Enron's stock began to slide faster and faster and the centre could not hold. In an interconnected world, news of the troubles was spreading fast, leaving Enron employees holding the bag as the house of cards that they had built began to collapse.

It was late 2001 and the end of an era. In a few short months, Enron would be bankrupt. The collapse took everyone by surprise, particularly those who knew the company best. I was surprised by how quickly things were unfolding. The mighty Enron, the company that had always seemed able to pull a rabbit out of a hat at just the right time, was going down. By this point, I had already moved to New York City to start a hedge fund with a classmate from my MBA school. I called my friend Patrick, who was still working for Enron, to see what was going on there. Patrick was a portfolio manager for an Enron-sponsored internal hedge fund that took positions on both the long and short side of energy stocks. When I asked if the rumours about Enron's demise were true, his response was "Come on, Stephenson, you worked here, you know what a house of cards the place is.... Right now, I'm shorting Enron stock within my portfolio." This was unbelievable—an Enron employee was betting against the company that employed him. It was survival of the fittest at this point.

I could not have known it at the time, but within seven years the same sort of thing was going to happen again. This time, I was going to be an eyewitness not merely to corporate greed gone wild but to the near total collapse of the global financial system. As with Enron, the global collapse was one that almost no one saw coming. However, the crisis of 2008 had repercussions that would be much more dramatic and far reaching than the chain of events that followed the Enron implosion.

BEAR STEARNS: HISTORY REPEATS ITSELF

In late March 2008, a sense of despair permeated Bear Stearns's world headquarters in downtown Manhattan. How had it happened? Wasn't it just a couple of weeks earlier that Alan "Ace" Greenberg, the chair of the firm's executive committee, had described the possibility of a liquidity crunch hitting the eighty-five-year-old investment banking firm as "totally ridiculous"? Yet it had happened, and the world of Wall Street would be decimated.

It was Enron all over again. Bear Stearns was a storied investment bank that, since its founding in 1923, had been one of the most successful franchises on Wall Street, becoming the fifth-largest investment bank in the U.S., with more than fifteen thousand employees in twenty-five offices around the world. Like many of its competitors, it bought and sold equities and debt products for customers on its own account, and provided advisory services on mergers and other corporate transactions. On the street, the firm was known as tough and scrappy—even a little arrogant.

There had been rumours about troubles at Bear Stearns for weeks—that it was running out of cash. Large institutions were yanking trades away, afraid the company would leave them in the lurch if it went under. A crisis of confidence was plaguing the firm, sending its stock crashing from a high of more than $133 per share down to less than $10 the week before it was taken over. But all of that was old news. A week after its stock fell below $10, the firm was bought for the bargain price of $2 a share by JPMorgan Chase, a rival headquartered around the block.

Faced with a crisis of confidence, a firm can only hope and pray that it subsides. It can try to sell assets in an attempt to raise cash to meet its obligations. But these activities take time and time is not on your side in a panic. Bear Stearns had no choice but to accept whatever it could get for the firm once the death spiral began.

Bear Stearns was only the first domino to fall in a series of events that would rock the financial world. It would wipe out more than $34 trillion in stockholders' equity globally. It would precipitate soaring unemployment levels. It would decimate the savings of hundreds of millions of people and send real estate values tumbling.

With some of the largest and most prestigious financial firms in the world gone or merged into unrecognizable forms or becoming wards of the state, the corporate landscape would be changed forever. The crisis touched every corner of the world, with Europe falling harder and faster than even the U.S., the epicentre of the disaster. Countries such as Iceland would be economically ruined, Europeans would be screaming for regulation. The ideology of free enterprise capitalism would fall under unprecedented scrutiny and a new world economic order would emerge.

I had seen the hijacking of the American Dream by greedy executives before on a smaller scale with Enron. Financial crises never end quickly—they grow and envelop a whole industry or, in this case, the Western world. So I started digging in. I wanted to make sure this time I would profit from this disaster, that something good would come out of it. I read everything I could on the meltdown, on central banking and on money flows. My assumptions came from what I had learned at Enron—namely, that as the crisis unfolded it would claim more victims before things settled down.

FOR SALE

While Enron had structured off-balance-sheet vehicles to hide under-performing assets from the prying eyes of analysts, Wall Street did it one better. It sold your house right out from under you without you even knowing it.

Greedy bankers, foolhardy buyers, enabling politicians and a deal that was just too good to be true helped fuel the greatest asset bubble the world has ever seen. Bubbles are not new to the world of investments. They happen whenever investors take complete leave of their senses and bid prices up to stratospheric levels, beyond the levels dictated by the fundamentals of the investment.

From 2002 to 2007, residential housing became the new product that Wall Street was peddling. With a world-class marketing engine like Wall Street behind real estate, a bubble certainly couldn't be long in forming. Wall Street was helped along by the U.S. president, Congress and the chairman of the Federal Reserve, the U.S.'s central bank—all of them hell bent on increasing home ownership—and by a public that yearned for a sure thing on their investments. Acting independently, but with utter self-interest, they managed to create the biggest financial catastrophe the world has ever known.

Owning a home is a key part of the American Dream. But now, it wasn't just the American people who loved the idea of home ownership—the American government was encouraging it as well.

To help more Americans become homeowners, the government put in place several policies to encourage people to take the plunge. The first was making mortgage interest tax deductible. The second was the creation of two mammoth firms—Fannie Mae and Freddie Mac—to help facilitate mortgage lending. Another major initiative was the 1997 Community Reinvestment Act, which made it a requirement for banks to meet the credit needs of what was called the "entire community." The U.S. Federal Reserve also helped encourage home ownership by holding down interest rates. Together, these laws and policies created the perfect climate to encourage both the naïve and the sophisticated to throw caution to the wind.

At the centre of the coming storm were Fannie Mae and Freddie Mac. The mission of these two enormous, government-sponsored enterprises was simple: grease the wheels of the residential mortgage market so more Americans could own a home. Rather than lending directly to consumers, they worked with banks and brokers to ensure that mortgages were available at reasonable rates. To do this, they provided funds directly to other financial institutions, which in turn lent the money out to consumers. Throughout the 1990s, Congress encouraged Fannie and Freddie to guarantee a wider range of loans. Keeping interest rates low, encouraging questionable lending practices and appointing their buddies to key posts at these agencies were just some of the ways that the

American government encouraged, perhaps unwittingly, the formation of a massive speculative bubble in residential real estate.

Franklin Raines, who had been President Bill Clinton's White House budget director, was appointed by him to head Fannie Mae. Under his leadership, Fannie Mae began a pilot project in 1999 to ease the credit requirements of the loans that Fannie Mae acquired from banks. Over the years, both Fannie Mae and Freddie Mac expanded their loans and continued to support the U.S. government's goal of increasing home ownership. The job was a good one for Raines, who in 2003 pocketed more than $20 million in total compensation. In 2004, when the U.S. Securities and Exchange Commission began investigating alleged accounting irregularities at Fannie Mae, Raines took early retirement. It was claimed that Fannie Mae's earnings were overstated and losses were shifted, or hidden, in ways that allowed senior executives of the firm to earn large bonuses. By 2008, Fannie and Freddie were guarantors of fully half the residential mortgages in America—worth some $5.1 trillion. They would have lapped up many of the most toxic mortgage-backed securities that the wizards of Wall Street were having trouble selling to anyone else. Meanwhile, the allegations of fraud at the top continued to swirl around Fannie Mae.

Back on Wall Street, the hunt was on for the next new thing now that the salad days of the dot-com mania were over. To keep posting healthy profits and to keep their stock prices on the rise, the wizards needed to find the next great bull market and jump aboard. Residential real estate was perfect. It was an enormous market, widely perceived as safe and stable. With a little financial hocus pocus, they could create the perfect product. The question was simple: how?

The solution the wizards came up with was to "securitize" real estate—that is, to turn a pool of mortgages into a security that could be freely traded in the bond market. Securitization in itself was nothing new, having been used since the 1970s to convert the cash flows from student loans, credit cards and car loans into bonds that pension fund managers or others could buy. This time around, the only difference was that it would be applied to residential mortgages.

To investors, this was a delicious new opportunity. After years of strong economic growth and low inflation rates, the interest rates a pension fund could earn holding a portfolio of investment-grade bonds was pretty low, ranging from around 3 per cent to 5½ per cent. Pension funds faced a huge problem: they had lots of pensioners but not enough return to fund their benefits. And getting 3 or 4 per cent on a government bond wasn't going to earn a pension fund enough money to pay its retirees. One solution for pension funds was to allocate a greater percentage of their portfolios toward stocks, but that entailed taking on more risk. To an investment banker, a problem like this was really an opportunity in disguise. Throw in enough smarts, toss in a little securitization and—presto—you've got a whole new line of business.

But to demonstrate to money managers that these new securities were low risk, investment bankers needed to have the products rated as investment grade by the various rating agencies. If Moody's, Fitch or S&P were to issue an investment-grade rating for their bonds, it would be the ticket to unlocking the institutional marketplace. An investment-grade rating was the gold standard for bond ratings: it would allow these new mortgage-backed bonds to pass muster with investment committees at the pension funds, mutual funds and sovereign wealth funds around the world.

THE CASH STARTS COMIN'

Money talks, but big money screams. For the rating agencies, rating structured products, such as mortgage-backed securities, was big business. By 2007, rating agencies were earning 50 per cent of their revenues from bonds backed by car loans, subprime mortgages and the associated derivative products linked to them.

But part of what made rating these structured products so difficult was their complexity; some contained as many as a million underlying mortgages in a single product. For a rating to be assigned, the products needed to be analyzed by the rating agencies. But how could they understand products as complicated as this? After all, Wall Street had legions of the smartest minds in business backstopped by a phalanx of geeks and nerds crunching out complicated mathematical models. The complexity was intentional. The wizards of Wall Street had designed their products to be as confusing and complicated as possible so that clients and rating agencies would avoid asking the obvious question: does the structure even make sense?

The wizards soon discovered that if they sliced and diced enough mortgages together—some of questionable quality and others, slightly better—it made quite a cocktail. Follow up that strategy by mixing in mortgages from all over the country and it effectively would be impossible for anyone to really figure out what was in these structures. Of course, it didn't hurt that the investment banks were luring away all of the best and brightest analysts from the rating agencies with big dough, creating what amounted to a brain drain. It was Enron all over again, but instead of overly complicated natural gas structures, these were complicated residential mortgages structures.

To keep a yield-hungry client base happy, the investment bankers went on a hiring spree. They needed plenty of salesmen and lots of math, economics and physics geeks to churn out more of these complicated products. And churn them out they did. According to *The Economist*, by mid-June 2008, there were $2.5 trillion in outstanding asset-backed securities in the U.S. market. But there was an obvious and fatal flaw in the wizards' work: it was based on the assumption that house prices would continue to move higher.

From 2005 to 2007, this market exploded. Sick of low yields on government treasury securities, investors around the globe lined up to purchase these newfangled products, which seemed to offer a perfect combination of a reasonable return with very low risk. By 2007, major investment banks were all in on it. The British, French and Swiss all bought or sold this stuff in spades. Little did they know that a tidal wave of toxic sludge was about to wash up on both sides of the Atlantic.

Not content with merely securitizing a bunch of mortgages, investment bankers created even more ways to sell off a little piece of the American Dream. Mortgages were pooled and then those pools were further split in slices—or tranches, as they are called on the Street—according to how risky they were. Investors looking to get a little more risk and return could speculate by buying a tranche from the bottom-of-the-barrel BBB-rated sludge. And if those lowest rated mortgage-backed securities gave cause for worry, the bankers had created a way to hedge, or make side bets, on their financial health as well.

And as it turned out, the side bets were more than merely a sideshow. The premiums paid on them provided investment banks with much-needed cash flows that could be repackaged into new bonds to feed the hungry beast. The international demand for this investment-grade paper was so strong that Wall Street had actually started creating products out of the side bets against other bonds they had issued to satisfy this need. This was an astounding bit of financial sleight of hand. In the end, Wall Street didn't even need a homebuyer with lousy credit to float a new bond. All it needed was investors to take side bets against the health of their existing bonds and, like magic, new products were created out of thin air.

Demand for these supposedly safe securities was insatiable and the wizards that worked in this new area of structured finance had it good. At Merrill Lynch, a separate reporting channel was even created within the firm, becoming a world unto itself. No longer did the wizards working in structured finance have to report to the head of the fixed-income group. In the new world, the wizards had a separate reporting structure that led directly to the CEO's office. And pay reflected it. Top bankers could easily make $8 to $12 million a year at the height of the market.[1] By June 2008, some $2.5 trillion worth of asset-backed securities was still floating around and most of it was tied to subprime mortgages in the U.S. And the market for side bets? It grew to a staggering $30 trillion, or more than two times America's annual gross domestic product.

Luckily, there was no shortage of people looking for a deal. With the U.S. government bending over backwards to make it easy to buy a home, just about everyone was a candidate for a mortgage—or five. In the new era of easy money, those who had poor credit, the so-called subprime candidates, were fair game. HCL Finance, a leading independent mortgage lender, started proudly advertising a signature loan it called the NINJA—an acronym for no income, no job, no assets.

At the height of the frenzy that followed, mortgages were issued over the phone in sixty seconds or less—guaranteed. Convicts, illegal immigrants and people on welfare all were potential candidates for home ownership. It didn't matter if they had credit or not. Mortgages were issued without any documentation, even to people the lending companies knew had provided false information on their applications. All that mattered was that they wanted to own a home. In America, there was always a way.

THE FIX IS IN

All this easy credit had a predictable outcome: it forced up the value of real estate higher than it might otherwise have gone, all the way to unsustainable levels. People were buying three, four houses—all with no money down. Anyone who could fog a mirror could be a homeowner in the U.S.

Then, all of a sudden, things changed. Some of the subprime mortgages that had initially offered low introductory teaser rates started to reset to higher—higher than normal—interest. In some cases, monthly mortgage payments tripled overnight. Some homeowners who found themselves with negative equity in their homes—their mortgages worth more than their home's value—walked away.

"For sale" signs began springing up on lawns across America, and house prices across the country began to fall. Homeowners who had loaded up on the easy credit and bought three and four properties, often with little or nothing down, were unable to carry their mortgages and started selling, hoping to get out before the music stopped.

Shares in homebuilders and mortgage finance companies started falling hard as investors speculated that tough times might be around the corner. Shares in banks, as well as in Freddie Mac and Fannie Mae, fell as the market became concerned about rising default rates in its mortgage portfolios, reckoning that this would mean that the banks would be either earning less fee income from their portfolio of mortgages, incurring more costs, or both. No matter how you sliced it, it was bad news.

Shares of banks sold off hard. Banks are a low-margin business made attractive by the tremendous amount of leverage they use to generate profits. A typical bank has leverage of ten to one, meaning it has nine dollars of borrowed money for every dollar of its own. When a bank gets into trouble, leverage becomes a huge millstone around its neck. On Wall Street, the problem of leverage was worse, with the typical investment bank being leveraged thirty to one. This meant there was almost no room to manoeuvre if its share price got into trouble.

The glue that holds the banking industry together is confidence. If a bank loses the confidence of either depositors or shareholders, a run on the bank can ensue. And once a bank gets into trouble, it can't call in its loans fast enough to pay off depositors and quickly becomes insolvent. Even the merest whiff of a problem with a bank's capital base can cause depositors to panic, leaving an institution at the mercy of either the regulator or frightened depositors.

All of a sudden, the complicated structures that the wizards had so shamelessly sold started failing and a once burning hot market turned ice cold. In some cases, the first loss on these securities had to be eaten by the investment banks that sold them. In others, collateral had to be tossed in to support the products. Just as the executives at Enron had thought of themselves as the smartest guys in the room, the banks' own hubris blinded them to the facts—that banks and investment banks had no business lending money to people who had no hope of paying them back. Once the market figured out that Wall Street had lied, that trillions of dollars' worth of products had been created on the flawed assumption that residential real estate prices always go up, investors were furious.

Arrogance, greed and short-term thinking were about to signal the end of Wall Street as we knew it. Investors who had bought these products based on the promises of investment bankers who assured them the likelihood of a loss was small sold in frustration. Unsurprisingly, there weren't many takers. Hedge fund players, the sharks of the investment industry, smelled blood and went in for the kill. Which firms had issued the most mortgage-backed paper in the last few years? They sold short the shares of these companies, sending the stock market into a tailspin along the way.

Back in Toronto, my quote screen was a sea of red. Troy, my trader, was in my office screaming that "the market monkey is going crazy" as desperate investors rushed toward the exits. Everybody was trying to get into cash, but there weren't enough buyers. From September to December 2008, our morning meetings were pretty much the same. The numbers were sobering. Shanghai was down 5.4 per cent in overnight trading and the stock index futures on New York were pointing toward the Dow being down 4.5 per cent. On occasion, it turned out to be better than expected, other days, much worse. From mid-September to mid-November 2008, the Toronto stock exchange posted fourteen of the seventeen worst single-day declines. Ever.

When the levee finally broke, and the sea of lies and broken promises came rushing in, global stock markets exacted swift and painful retribution on any company that had had a hand in the subprime mess. The first to fall were Fannie Mae and Freddie Mac, which had gobbled up some of the most toxic of the mortgage-backed products Wall Street was selling. First, their stocks sold off hard and then their bonds came under attack. Would they really be forced into bankruptcy and renege on repaying bondholders? Some big players owned Fannie and Freddie bonds globally, including the Russians, who had invested more than US$900 billion in them. Even though Fannie and Freddie were technically not controlled by the U.S. government, their bonds were marketed as if they carried an implicit guarantee from the United States government to honour them. With the stock prices of Fannie and Freddie circling the drain, the U.S. government stepped in and made these two behemoths enter conservatorship. The government chose to make good on the firms' implicit government backing, rather than lose all credibility globally by reneging on their debts.

Next, investors started focusing on American International Group (AIG), the largest insurance company in the world. Over the years, AIG had discovered it could make a lot of money by selling insurance against the likelihood of corporate bankruptcy. In effect, AIG was the house for all of those side bets that everyone on Wall Street was making to hedge their positions on the mortgage-backed products they were buying. If an investor was going to buy a mortgage-backed bond issued by Merrill Lynch, he could get AIG to write an insurance policy that would cover the losses on that bond if Merrill got into trouble. But now AIG was the one in trouble. If it failed, the whole cross-linking of the global financial services sector could come unstuck. To prevent a total meltdown of the global financial system, the American government felt it had no choice but to nationalize AIG.

A DELICATE BALANCE

With the U.S. Federal Reserve and the Treasury Department taking an ad hoc approach to picking winners and losers, the market was becoming more desperate by the minute. Was there a game plan? Who owned what? Which company was the linchpin that would cause the whole global financial system to come crashing down?

The global financial crisis entered a dangerous new phase. Banks, the grease of the country's economic engine, were hoarding whatever cash they had in a desperate bid to stay afloat. As banks stopped lending to one another, the once free flowing credit markets ground to a halt like a clogged artery. Global economic collapse was heading down the pike. Fast.

The time for ad hoc fixes was over. America was the epicentre of the problem and it was America that had to rally the world with a solution. The Europeans had started off co-operating with one another, but once the problem became severe, they panicked and started to bail out their leading companies. The British nationalized Royal Bank of Scotland, and tiny Iceland begged the Russians and the International Monetary Fund for a massive bailout to save its economy from complete and total ruin.

In the U.S., things were moving fast. Congress had been told that the system needed fixing immediately. After much toing and froing, it finally passed the Troubled Asset Relief Program, or TARP, a $700 billion rescue plan for America's financial institutions. The nationalization of AIG, as well as Fannie and Freddie and the passage of TARP, all occurred within two weeks. In this window, Congress also passed legislation to extend deposit insurance to cover $3.4 trillion in money market funds, the Securities and Exchange Commission temporarily banned short selling of more than nine hundred financial services stocks and Congress called former executives to the Hill to testify about the crisis. Meanwhile, the stock, bond, currency and commodity markets continued in free fall.

Everyone was selling whatever they could, as quickly as they could. When the dust began to settle, trillions of dollars of investors' capital had been wiped out. Huge gaps were apparent in the global financial system and investors were completely and utterly shell shocked.

AMERICA THE FALLEN

The financial costs for the bailout have been staggering. But even more devastating has been the loss of America's reputation as a global financial leader. Gone are the days of the U.S. lecturing the world on the merits of free market capitalism. In one fell swoop, America transformed capitalism—as it had championed it through most of the last century—into a newfangled form of socialism. America's biggest and best institutions, the ones that had shown such impressive earnings growth and led their benchmark stock index, the S&P 500, higher, had been reduced to being wards of the state.

Like its citizens, America has been living on borrowed money for some time. Since 1990, the U.S. has moved from being the largest creditor nation to being the largest debtor nation in the world. Americans consume too much, produce too little and save almost nothing. To finance its bad habits, the U.S. needs to sell $60 billion of U.S. treasuries every month just to balance its chequebook. Sluggish wage growth is another problem. From 2000 to 2007, U.S. wages grew at an average annual rate of 3.3 per cent, but when this number is adjusted for inflation, real wage growth over the period was a paltry 0.5 per cent. Making matters worse, the bottom 60 per cent of American households had less income in 2007 than they did in 2000, with the top 40 per cent of American households pulling up the average.

American consumers are losing big on their real estate investments, their employers are closing down shop and the stock market is down big. For the baby boom generation, this had been a bitter pill to swallow. First there was the tech wreck. Then the same bunch of charlatans that sold this group an inflated pets.com stock sold their houses out from under them and cratered their investments, all in a vicious, one-two combination. American investors are reeling and will need to add years to their working lives to dig themselves out of this hole.

For many Americans, job losses will be merely the first shoe to drop. Unlike Canada and the United Kingdom, which have government-run health care systems, American health insurance is administered by private corporations, leaving 46 million Americans without health coverage. While the U.S. government does provide Medicare to those over sixty-five or disabled, only bankruptcy allows other individuals to qualify for assistance under the program.

The savings rate of the average American is close to zero. A massive trade deficit and total household and national debts totaling $51 trillion will give America very little room to manoeuvre in the lean times. But that is only part of the story. An enormous funding gap exists between what Social Security and Medicare have promised to deliver and the assets that they have to pay for it. Over a seventy-five-year horizon, the funding gap for Social Security, in today's dollars, is $4.3 trillion. For Medicare it is $8.7 trillion—an amount nowhere to be found on official U.S. debt books. Like Wall Street, the U.S. government simply has slid inconvenient problems off its balance sheet, out of view.

America has been living beyond its means for decades. The low-interest-rate policy that former Federal Reserve Chairman Alan Greenspan initiated and that Congress, as well as the administration, supported served only one purpose—to promote massive borrowing. People used the easy money of the early 2000s to speculate in stocks, bonds and real estate.

In 1991, Japan faced a situation similar to the current one in the U.S. After five years of frenzied growth in real estate and stock prices, it entered a deflationary spiral that has lasted until this day. As in the U.S., easy money and loose credit policies conspired to create a massive bubble in Japanese stocks and real estate. When it popped, Japan never recovered. The bubble in American housing and stocks has been growing for twenty years as opposed to five, which raises the question: could America be the next Japan?

Japan is a land of savers and America is a land of spenders. When its crisis erupted, Japan's savings rate was a healthy 16 to 17 per cent. America's current household savings rate hovers around zero. With $1.3 billion more coming into the nation's coffers each and every day than is going out, the Japanese economy is currently in a surplus position. In the U.S., the situation is the exact opposite, with $2 billion leaving its coffers daily to finance massive American consumption.

America will always matter to the world, but never as much as it did. Its most successful corporations have turned out to be nothing more than an elaborate ruse. In the aftermath of this crisis, its government and consumer finances are in shambles and its pre-eminence in question. America is strong, its people resourceful. They will need all of that and more in the years ahead.

3

ASIAN EXPRESS

The world's economic future belongs to Asia—the continent with the people, the money and the work ethic to drive the global economy forward for the next century. Over the last decade, the economies of India, China and Southeast Asia have been expanding at a mind-boggling rate. The results have been nothing short of amazing. Throughout the region, the inflation-adjusted growth rate over the last seven years ranged from a low of 5.0 per cent in Thailand to a high of 10.2 per cent in China. In the same time frame, the economic growth rate was 2.9 per cent in Canada and 2.6 per cent in the U.S. Yet despite overwhelming evidence of Asia's ascent, skepticism runs deep among North American investors.

THE ASIAN MIRACLE HITS A SPEED BUMP

It's difficult not to have a sense of déjà vu. Wasn't it just a decade ago that global stock markets were in full retreat because of a financial crisis originating in Asia? This time, America is the epicentre of the meltdown, but many people are left wondering: won't America drag down Asia too? But today things *are* different and the roles have been completely reversed.

During the 1980s and 1990s, the economies of Thailand, Malaysia, Singapore, Indonesia and South Korea were growing rapidly—

collectively they were dubbed the "Asian economic miracle." Global investors, always on the hunt to make quick and easy profits, were attracted to the region because of its impressive economic growth. With annual growth rates in the 8 to 12 per cent range, Asia was ground zero for lots of *hot* foreign money. As the money rushed in, real estate and stock prices went higher. Much higher.

When you blow too much air into a balloon, it bursts. Too much money chasing too few investment alternatives can do the same thing to an economy. With economic growth on a tear, investors from around the world bid up the prices for stocks and real estate in Southeast Asia. In July 1997, the bubble finally burst. Investors started rushing for the exits, sending currencies, real estate and stocks crashing down. Since then, a decade of sound government policies has put Southeast Asia on a solid financial footing and made the region a potential global lifeboat for the West—a stunning transformation.

On a recent trip to Southeast Asia, I made a stopover in Seoul, South Korea. Seoul is a modern, affluent city of 10 million people. Throw in the neighbouring port city of Incheon and some of the surrounding towns and greater Seoul is the second-largest metropolitan region in the world. Everywhere you look are glittering skyscrapers, wide boulevards and impressive vistas. South Korea is also home to industrial giants such as Hyundai, LG Electronics and Samsung. These household names have helped make Seoul Asia's fourth-richest city.

On a stroll through downtown Seoul it's difficult to imagine that just ten years ago, this city, and indeed most of Southeast Asia, was embroiled in its own economic storm. But the lessons from the Asian financial crisis have been learned. And in the process, the region has been transformed, so much so that today it is the sound finances of these emerging markets that are being called upon to bail out the submerging markets in the West. The tables have turned.

In the Asian financial crisis, banks, businesses and currencies collapsed in short order as investors panicked and sold. In the aftermath of this disaster, it became apparent why this had happened. Loose regulation of the banking industry and weak monetary policies allowed credit to expand at a breakneck pace. When the extent of the shoddy finances and weak government oversight became apparent, capital flowed out of the region in a hurry and desperate governments went searching for bailouts. With little in the way of foreign currency reserves to draw upon, the central banks were powerless to stop sharp declines in their currencies. As the region's currencies tumbled, foreigners continued to sell their holdings, further depressing the economies and currencies.

Foreign currency reserves are like a government piggy bank. When a country sells more abroad than it imports, it builds up reserves of dollars, yen or other currencies. That piggy bank can come in handy in times of trouble to help fund development projects at home or abroad or to be spent defending the national currency from attacks by speculators. In 1997, the region's piggy banks were nearly empty, leaving local governments with little choice but to watch and wait as their currencies plummeted.

With hundreds of billions at stake, urgent global co-operation was needed to stem the growing financial crisis, and the International Monetary Fund (IMF) was called in. The crisis had enveloped the region, and the world, within a matter of weeks. Urgent action was needed. South Korea, Indonesia and Thailand were in the worst shape and desperately needed the IMF to stabilize their currencies and restore confidence in the region. It obliged with an initial US$40 billion bailout program, but strings were attached. Deficits needed to be reduced, insolvent banks had to fail, oversight of all financial activities needed to be implemented and interest rates had to rise for the money to flow.

The causes of the Asian crisis were many, but in retrospect the single biggest factor was a massive credit bubble that burst. Large quantities of readily available credit helped push the price of real estate and other assets to unsustainable levels. Once asset prices started to collapse, borrowers stuck with overvalued assets started to default on their loans—many of which were in U.S. dollars.

The parallels with the current financial crisis couldn't be more obvious. Loose monetary policies, weak banking oversight and greedy speculators helped to inflate a bubble in Southeast Asian real estate and stocks. In the United States, the loose monetary policies of the era presided over by former Federal Reserve Chairman Alan Greenspan, weak oversight of over-the-counter derivative transactions and greedy bankers contributed to a stunning collapse. But rather than letting insolvent banks fail, America has propped them up. America's deficit is soaring and nobody in America seems to know the full extent of the problem, let alone how to regulate it. But the major difference between then and now is that today the mess is a whole lot bigger and the American currency hasn't collapsed, at least not yet.

ASIA NOW

In downtown Bangkok, partially completed buildings covered in mould are painful reminders of a real estate bubble that burst a decade ago. But gone today is the sense of panic that was palpable when Asia was at the centre of the storm. While the Asian stock markets have moved in lockstep with international markets, outside the trading rooms is relative calm.

Ten years ago, Asia was engulfed in a crisis from overzealous liberalization of its financial sector and other self-inflicted wounds. Today, all the major Asian countries, except India, have small ratios of public debt to gross domestic product (GDP), giving the government substantial flexibility to cut taxes or boost public spending. According to *The Economist*, "Total domestic debt (private and public) fell to 143% of GDP in emerging Asia in 2007, compared with 251% of GDP in America."[1]

While the current financial crisis will undoubtedly lap up on Asian shores, the global financial crisis that is consuming the West is just a passing curiosity in Asia. For Asia, the current crisis is like a major storm sweeping through a neighbouring community, you know it's going to reach you, but for now you're resigned to just watch with curious detachment as it unfolds.

The transformation of the economies of Malaysia, Thailand, Indonesia and South Korea, as well as the other countries in Southeast Asia, is largely complete. Indonesia and South Korea cleaned up their corporate governance and improved government regulation of financial institutions. Foreign currency reserves have exploded over the last eleven years and now sit at a staggering $4 trillion across the region. A previous over-reliance on trade with the U.S. and the fickle capital flows of foreign investors have refocused attention on a made-in-Asia solution.

When a recovery begins in the United States, U.S. growth initially will be anaemic. The U.S. banking system is so severely impaired that it will take years before it is repaired. The American government and consumer are both so severely indebted that it will be years before they can dig themselves out of this mess. U.S. consumer confidence has plunged and America's global leadership role is in doubt. The free market capitalism that America championed as Asia was emerging has blown apart at the seams as the rot from within has been exposed.

With the West nearly bankrupt, the solution to the current crisis can occur *only* with help from Asia, where savings rates are high and government coffers are overflowing. The leaders of the world's chief economies have been meeting non-stop since the current crisis began. From America and Britain the message is the same: this is a global problem and therefore requires a global solution.

China, with a domestic savings rate of more than 35 per cent and $1.9 trillion in foreign currency reserves, is a logical saviour. China has responded to the cry for assistance by announcing a massive $586 billion stimulus package geared toward *domestic* infrastructure projects. Rather than heed the international calls for direct cash infusions in multilateral organizations, such as the IMF, China's response has been a straightforward *no*. While in Lima, Peru, for a meeting of the leaders of the G20 group of nations, Chinese president Hu Jintao put it this way: "The steady and relatively fast economic development in China is in itself a major contributor to upholding international financial stability and promoting world economic development."[2]

Prodigious savings, a reformed and stable banking sector and a focus on labour productivity have already made Asia and the emerging world *the* driver of global economic growth. While undoubtedly there will be bumps along the road, Asia is well prepared to withstand the current economic storm.

Asia has what the world needs for it to get out of the current crisis—the money, the people and the stability. The last decade has seen a dramatic shift in the global economic playing field. While Americans spent their way into poverty, Asians dug their way out of poverty and into a prosperous future. America is a land of resilient and flexible people. All of that will be severely tested in the years that lie ahead. In the meantime, the future is in Asia, not in America, whose problems have brought the world to the brink of collapse.

ASIA ON THE MOVE

Many North Americans have a tainted view of Asia. Surely, we think, there must be some kind of *angle* that explains its rapid rise. Many of us think the news reports touting Asia's rapid rise have glossed over how it *really* achieved this success. I've heard people suggest that Asia is competitive only because it exploits its workers. They say its culture stifles innovation and relies on stealing other people's intellectual property. The place is horribly polluted and corruption runs rampant. When economic growth in the West slows, rapid growth will be over for Asia. While there is some truth in all of these statements, Asia is more fascinating, exciting and entrepreneurial than you might ever imagine. When you begin to open your mind to Asia, you start to see the true power behind the numbers, the people.

Asia, like America, is diverse. It simply defies categorization. The continent is massive both in physical size—at 44.579 million square kilometres it is more than 82 per cent larger than North America—and in the number and diversity of its people. The continent is home to 44 per cent of the world's people. India is the world's largest democracy and China is its most populous country.

I'm used to the four-hour journey between Toronto and Montreal on VIA Rail, but that hardly prepared me for riding the rails in Asia. In Japan, the bullet train is a truly first-class way to travel. And Shanghai's Maglev high-speed train whisks weary travellers from Pudong international airport to the city's subway terminus at a clip of 430 kilometres an hour.

Everything about Asia challenges your beliefs and leaves you amazed. I saw no hint of the stereotyped communist bureaucracy in Vietnam, where a flight was arranged for me and my ticket upgraded at eleven at night while I was transferring through Ho Chi Minh City airport en route to Seoul for a few days. Talk about a winning customer-service attitude. Near where I was staying in Beijing were three other hotels, each with a different car dealership in its lobby: Rolls-Royce, Maserati or BMW. Chinese technology experts are being solicited by headhunters for jobs in California and London.

To keep their best knowledge workers, Asian firms, like those in the West, *must* pay world-scale wages. While low-skill, low-wage work exists throughout Asia, these manufacturing jobs nonetheless offer a substantially better life than does subsistence farming. Many employers of low-skilled labourers provide them with room and board and three square meals a day.

In China, property rights have been enshrined constitutionally. And in recent years, Chinese firms have taken legal action against one another for intellectual patent infringement. Corruption, while still an issue, is no worse than it is anywhere else. And as Asia's stake in the global economy increases, the pressure to make its society more open and transparent only increases.

Pollution is a major concern in Asia. But the flip side to that is that it is also a major opportunity for Asians and others to try to solve. When I was in China in 2007, university professors and government officials talked to the group of North American investors I was with about their efforts to monitor and improve air and water pollution in China. Contrary to what you have heard, this is an issue that the Chinese government and ordinary folk know about and are concerned about.

Wherever you go, Asia confronts your stereotypes. The buildings are more magnificent than you can imagine; the people are friendly and they genuinely do their best to help you. There is great hope, huge progress and much more to be done. Asia is the future for those of us bold enough and open-minded enough to grab hold of it.

FIGURE 3.1 Asia's Economic Growth Explodes

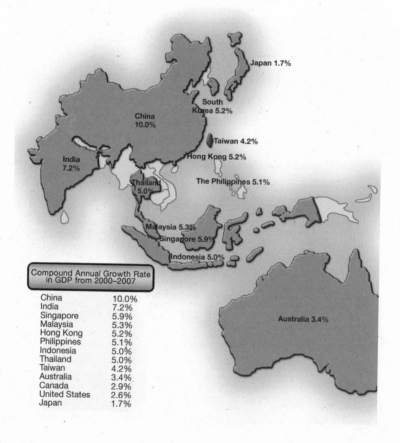

Compound Annual Growth Rate in GDP from 2000–2007	
China	10.0%
India	7.2%
Singapore	5.9%
Malaysia	5.3%
Hong Kong	5.2%
Philippines	5.1%
Indonesia	5.0%
Thailand	5.0%
Taiwan	4.2%
Australia	3.4%
Canada	2.9%
United States	2.6%
Japan	1.7%

THE ASIAN TIGERS BEGIN TO ROAR

Japan was the first economy in the region to experience rapid growth. Next, beginning in the 1960s, four countries known collectively as the "Asian Tigers" (Hong Kong, Taiwan, Singapore and South Korea) began a process of rapid economic growth and industrialization, which was largely complete by the early 1990s. Rather than concentrating on spurring domestic demand, these countries, with plenty of cheap labour, focused on export-led growth. America and other rich nations gobbled up all the toys and clothes they could find with *Made in Asia* labels. In the process, the region accumulated large foreign currency reserves and huge trade surpluses with the West.

The game plan that Japan had laid down was simple. It decided to develop its manufacturing prowess by exploiting its large pool of low-cost labour. As it developed and exported more, its national wealth increased. With increasing national wealth, it began to diversify out of lower value-added businesses such as steelmaking and into producing cars, cameras and computers. Many of us can remember the Datsun and other early Japanese cars. They had a reputation for being unreliable rust buckets. But nowadays, no one laughs at you for driving a Lexus. They'd be more likely to turn green with envy.

Successive waves of Asian countries have followed this model of increasing national wealth by starting with low-end consumer products such as clothing and then evolving to high-end consumer products. Taiwan, a small nation of 23 million people, is a high-tech manufacturing centre that is home to AAEON Technology Inc. and Acer, a manufacturer of computers and other information technology products. American citizens of Taiwanese origin have gone on to become the co-founders of companies as wide ranging as Nautica, which designs, makes and sells clothing, accessories and furniture, and YouTube and Yahoo, two hugely popular Internet companies.

The region continues to grow at an impressive clip, but today the growth is coming from Thailand, Vietnam, Malaysia, Indonesia and, of course; India and China. The business model these emerging Asian tigers are following is the same as the one pioneered by Japan more than fifty years ago.

BEYOND BOLLYWOOD

India is a staggeringly large country of 1.2 billion people and its population is growing at a rate of 1.4 per cent a year—a rate that is 45 per cent faster than that of the U.S. The British ruled India for two centuries, until it gained independence in 1947. Its first prime minister was Jawaharlal Nehru, a charismatic leader who advocated total independence from the British and socialism. Under his direction and later under the leadership of his daughter, Indira Gandhi, and grandson Rajiv Gandhi, India developed a strong public-sector presence in the economy. India's economic growth, despite its hulking bureaucracy, has been impressive, averaging 10.9 per cent a year for the past decade.

While the Asian tigers focused on export-led growth over the last thirty years, India's entrepreneurs have focused on increasing domestic consumption and on the information technology industry to gain a toehold on the world stage. While Indian call centres are what many of us think about when our computers suffer a glitch or we have a problem with a credit card, India is way beyond call centres. In fact, India has developed a very strong technology industry. Infosys Technologies Limited, one such global IT giant, develops software and provides consulting solutions. In 2008, Infosys had revenues of $4.176 billion, with North America accounting for 60 per cent of its sales.[3] Indian IT firms with a global reach also include Wipro Technologies, a leading provider of systems integration and outsourcing services, and Tata Consultancy Services.

India puts Hollywood to shame with its thriving movie industry, which cranks out more than eight hundred films a year—more than double the number Hollywood produces. So dominant is the

Indian film industry that, according to Indian entertainment writer Tanya Palta, it accounts for 73 per cent of all Asia-Pacific movie admissions.[4]

India's economic gains in the last ten years have been impressive, with the percentage of disposable income among citizens rising from 14 per cent in the 1960s to 29 per cent today. With more disposable income, Indian consumption has been marching higher and now stands at $421 billion annually, a figure estimated to reach $1.4 trillion by 2025, which would make India the fifth-largest consumer market in the world. With an emerging middle class that at last count included approximately 300 million consumers, India's continued growth will have a big impact on the global economy.

COMMERCIALISM AND CONFUCIUS

If India is important to the global economic picture, China is the end-game. For eighteen of the last twenty centuries, China was the dominant economic force in the world—and it will be again. China may be operating under a Communist political system, but its economy is anything but sleepy. The pace of growth and the economic progress that China has pulled off in only thirty years is truly staggering.

After the Chinese civil war in 1949, the Chinese Communist Party, under the leadership of Mao Zedong, came to power. Under Mao, China withdrew from the world as he crafted the country through various social and political programs such as the Cultural Revolution. That all changed with Mao's death in 1978, when Deng Xiaoping threw open the doors to economic progress by liberalizing the economy. In introducing his more liberal economic reforms for China, Deng Xiaoping famously said, "It doesn't matter if a cat is black or white, so long as it catches mice." That kind of practical, get-the-job-done attitude defines the China of today.

Permeating Chinese life and politics today are the teachings of Confucius, a philosopher born in 551 BC who stressed neutrality, familial loyalty, the respect of elders, and personal and governmental morality. According to Na Liu, a Chinese citizen and China analyst at Scotia Capital in Toronto, "China's Communist party is not a Stalinist party, as in Russia. It has been softened by Confucianism." In fact, pretty much everyone in China, particularly in the rural communities, adheres to this philosophy. The teachings of Confucius that stress being neutral and not going to extremes underpin Chinese culture as well as foreign and domestic affairs to this day.

By any measure, China's economy is a rip-roaring success. China has followed the model of export-led growth, exporting about 40 per cent of GDP. Increasingly, Chinese products are moving up the sophistication scale. In 2006, 42 per cent of total manufactured exports were electronic products, rather than T-shirts or Nike sneakers. The vastness of China's manufacturing capability cannot be understated. In the first ten months of 2008, China produced 119.3 million computers and 73.96 million televisions.[5] With huge annual earnings from abroad of approximately $1.3 trillion, China has amassed an impressive war chest of foreign currency reserves—a staggering $1.9 trillion, or about 28 per cent of the total global *foreign currency reserves*.[6]

Many people believe China's growth and rising affluence can be sustained only as long as Americans continue to flock to Wal-Mart to buy cheap Chinese-made goods. Nothing could be further from the truth. While the U.S. is an important market for China, its total exports to the U.S. represent a mere 7 per cent of Chinese GDP. The reality is that intra-Asian trade is far more important to China than trade with Western Europe or America. Manufacturing is an important source of employment in China, but only 6 per cent of the total Chinese workforce is engaged in export-oriented manufacturing. And while exports are an important contributor to Chinese growth, investment in property and infrastructure is the primary driver of the Chinese economy, accounting for 40 per cent of the total economic output.

Americans love to believe that China needs *them*, but the truth is exactly the opposite. After consuming beyond its means for decades, the U.S. now finds itself in the unenviable position of being the world's largest debtor nation. China, conversely, is the world's largest creditor nation and, as such, has been willing to finance American consumption by buying up America's treasury securities. America desperately needs China to support it and its debt-addicted citizens. If the Chinese ever decide that earning low rates of return on U.S. treasury securities is a bad deal and dump them on the open market, a collapse of the U.S. dollar won't be long in coming.

China has looked inward for most of its history. According to Liu, "The Great Wall of China is the symbol of the country's culture. It is there strictly for defensive purposes. The Chinese are interested in defense, not offense." For centuries, China has had the world's oldest culture and its largest economy; it has also been exceedingly self-reliant. The country boasts more than 180 cities with a million or more inhabitants, more than Western Europe and the United States combined.[7] China has 467 airports, 75,438 kilometres of railway track and more than 1.93 million kilometres of roads—all built to the highest standards in the world. The port of Shanghai, the largest in the world, handled 537 million tons of cargo in 2006. By comparison, Vancouver, Canada's largest and the fourth-largest port in North America, handles just 135 million tons a year. No matter how you slice it, China is a behemoth that is astounding the world.

Education is another area where China excels. For centuries, China had a system called *keju kaoshi*, which was a national examination system to promote government officials. In modern China, *keju* has been replaced with a national exam for college admission, but the legacy of scholarship remains.

Unlike North America, where it helps to know someone to get ahead, the Chinese annual national examination is a great leveller of socio-economic rank. Students from all walks of life who do well in the exam can find themselves at Beijing University, the country's top institute of higher education. From there, a good job awaits. In Chinese society, intellectuals and the learned class are the people of the highest social standing. It's a far cry from the North American system, where money is what matters and degrees have been bought rather than earned.

Chinese parents believe that intellectuals are on the highest rung of the social ladder and, with just one child per family, it's pretty certain that Junior will be studying—and studying hard. Many of China's best and brightest young people have studied in the West, learning how we do things here, before heading back home to help lead China forward. In China, as just about everywhere else, a degree from America's Harvard University is prized for an eventual career at home or abroad. Routinely, Chinese scholars are top of their class, regardless of where they attend university. Within China, the colleges and universities turn out more than six hundred thousand engineering graduates a year; America produces just seventy thousand.

FIGURE 3.2 China's Commodity Consumption

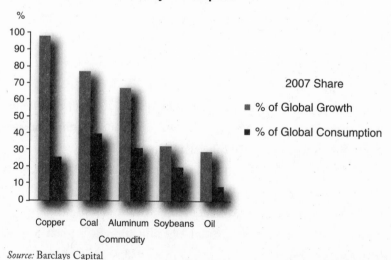

Source: Barclays Capital

A GLOBAL REACH

China in its truest sense is an *even bigger* economy than appears at first glance. The economic strength that is China also extends to a greater China beyond its borders, encompassing Taiwan and Hong Kong.

Taiwan, founded when the nationalist Kuomintang party of China fled to the island off the southeastern coast of China at the end of the Chinese civil war in 1949, now has a population of just 23 million but boasts the fifth-largest economy in Asia and has developed impressive national manufacturing champions such as AAEON Technology and Acer. To most Chinese, Taiwan, which recently renewed relations with the mainland, is the country's twenty-third province.

Hong Kong, a renowned banking and international business centre officially known as a special administrative zone, is another part of the greater China. If that weren't enough, around 70 million ethnic Chinese living abroad still maintain links with the mainland. Members of the Chinese diaspora are among the wealthiest citizens in their adopted homelands, which further extends the economic influence of China beyond its borders.

SOUTHEAST ASIA: ON THE MOVE

The economies of Malaysia, Vietnam, Indonesia and Thailand are also on the move. Collectively, they account for more than 400 million people and have foreign currency reserves in excess of $300 billion. Their nominal economic growth rates over the last seven years range from 5.0 per cent in Thailand to 16.3 per cent in Indonesia. According to *The Economist*, annual per capita income in Indonesia in 2007 was $1,840, in Thailand it was $7,816 and in the U.S. $45,841. With trade among nations increasing, there is a lot of room for these economies to expand and grow. Even if global growth were to slow, each of these four economies should be able to generate positive growth of at least 5 per cent a year—something the United States won't be able to do.

JAPAN—IN SEARCH OF AN OBSTETRICIAN

Japan, the country that started the Asian miracle, will show almost no growth in 2009. With an aging population, Japan has a poor demographic profile for a country hoping to flex its future economic muscle. But Japan, like most of its Asian neighbours, is a country of savers and investors. For decades, Japan has been building up enormous infrastructure to support its economy in the future. This strong infrastructure base has allowed Japan to become a world leader in automobiles, cameras and computers, while at the same time amassing foreign currency reserves of close to $1 trillion. While Japan has been caught in a deflationary spiral for more than fifteen years now, its large pool of savings will help to buffet Japan from the current crisis.

AN EMERGING MIDDLE CLASS

Globalization, while it has its detractors, is the single biggest force for lifting hundreds of millions out of poverty and, at the same time, improving living standards here at home. Globalization, especially in emerging markets, has for the last few decades been about labour productivity, but that is beginning to change. Increasingly, service industries and higher value-added manufactured products are replacing low-end manufactured items. As their economies developed, Taiwan and South Korea have been forced to produce higher value-added products such as electronics, cars and computers to compete with the emergence of China as a manufacturing centre. But China is experiencing a shift of its lower value-added manufacturing to Vietnam—a country with an average annual per capita income half of China's. Already, the major manufacturer Intel has announced plans to spend $300 million on a digital chips and computer part assembly plant.[8] Canon, a supplier of half the world's laser printers, has announced plans to construct the world's largest laser printer plant in Vietnam. Japan's evolution from low-end manufacturer to high-end manufacturer of Lexus and Toyota cars, with plants and marketing centres around the world, is the model the rest of Asia is following.

Globalization has been the single greatest wealth creation mechanism of our lifetime. While it has meant a retooling of our industrial base and a retraining of many of our citizens, it's impossible to deny the vast selection of low-cost goods available from around the world to us as consumers. Already, global growth is altering the business playing field. According to Mark Spelman of Accenture, a global management consultancy, companies from emerging markets will make up one-third of the *Fortune* 500 list of the world's largest firms within the next ten years. Already, sixty-two emerging market companies are on that list.

Our profligate ways are being financed by the excess foreign currency reserves from around the world, most of them from Asia. While we often find ourselves rushing to the store for another impulse purchase, the Asians tend to take a longer-term perspective. Nowhere is this more evident than in China, where the government operates under a series of five-year plans. While our infrastructure is crumbling, China has announced a $586 billion stimulus package, directed largely toward infrastructure development.[9]

Throughout Asia, similar enormous infrastructure booms are occurring that will support economic growth for decades. With their enormous foreign currency reserves and massive fiscal surpluses, Asian governments will be on an investment spree for the foreseeable future—everything from roads and rails to mobile phone networks. Already, China has more than 547 million phones in use within her borders. According to a report by the McKinsey Global Institute, the financial assets of state-owned Asian investment funds stand at $4.6 trillion. This figure is likely to increase to $7.3 trillion in the next five years assuming modest rates of growth.

On a recent trip to China, Graeme McCusker, executive vice-president of Ericsson China and an Irish expatriate who has lived all over the world, was frank when he told me, "The very best researchers that we have globally are Chinese—without a doubt." As the working world becomes increasingly knowledge based, China, with its emphasis on education, will be well situated to make the transition from a manufacturing-led economy to a service-led economy, a natural evolution as countries develop.

Smart people and hard work are helping to create a Chinese middle class. Since the vast majority of its people have yet to cash in on the boom, they have a drive and initiative rarely witnessed in North America. The percentage of China's population that is urban is 40.4 per cent, half that of the United States. According to the Chinese government, 250 million people are considered to be part of the middle class—defined as being able to afford a home, car or appliances. And that new, emerging middle class is starting to become a significant economic force in its own right. The growing middle class and the rapid industrialization of the country make China the single biggest force in the demand for many of the commodities that Canada is a world leader in producing.

Living standards around the world are rising, creating millions of new consumers each and every year. According to investment bank Goldman Sachs, the global middle class (living in households defined as having annual incomes ranging from $6,000 to $30,000) is increasing by 70 million people a year. It estimates that by 2030, another 2 billion people may have joined the ranks of the global middle class.

CALLING ON CANADA

So what does a future of continued Asian economic growth mean for Canada?

It means excellent news. We produce many of the commodities, such as copper, zinc, nickel, oil and water, that Asia will need to continue its explosive growth. The process of industrialization is highly metals intensive, energy intensive and water intensive—to mention just a few of the areas where Canada has a competitive advantage. By some estimates, the process of industrializing is more than twice as energy intensive as operating a country that is fully industrialized. This huge Asian expansion is creating unprecedented opportunities for companies with expertise in water, infrastructure, energy and base metals to profit from the coming boom. Unless you think that Asians will be content to forget about progress, you need to position your investments for continued global growth.

4
FINANCIAL FOLLIES

The lineup snaked around the block. When anxious depositors reached the front door, they found a two-page notice informing them that the bank was now closed.[1] The IndyMac Federal Bank in Pasadena, California, had closed three hours earlier than usual on that day in July 2008. Federal regulators had seized control of the bank. In what would amount at the time to the second-largest failure of a U.S. bank, IndyMac had been reeling from losses on mortgages made at the height of the housing boom. In the previous month, the bank had been bleeding deposits as nervous customers withdrew their funds. With the bank's stock trading for pennies a share, the Office of Thrift Supervision in Washington, the principal regulator for the bank, stepped in and transferred control to the Federal Deposit Insurance Corp.

A bank run is a scary thing to witness. People's life savings can be dashed in the blink of an eye as an institution they trusted folds in a matter of days, even hours. Banking is central to our whole way of life. From the credit cards we use to the mortgages we take out to buy homes, a modern economy simply can't function without a smoothly operating banking sector.

The crisis that started in America quickly grew to encompass almost all of the major financial institutions in the West. Few were spared the carnage as the rapid unwinding of leveraged bets gone bad decimated the capital structure of these firms. For some, salvation came in the form of a massive government bailout. In Canada, the combination of tighter regulatory oversight, a limited exposure to American subprime-related securities, and a careful balance between a strong national retail branch network and a smaller, less risk-seeking wholesale operation has put our banks in a unique position globally. The costs associated with the American, British and European bailouts have been enormous—costs that will be borne by taxpayers and institutions for decades to come. By sidestepping the crisis, Canada's banks will benefit from greatly weakened global competitors and Canadians ultimately will benefit from a stronger currency as our sound fiscal policies are rewarded.

BUSTED

The repercussions of the current crisis for the banking industry have been swift and dramatic. Banks have come under assault as the structured products linked to residential mortgages that the Wall Street wizards created have left investors wondering what banks really *own*, and what they *owe*. No one knows. As it turns out, the banks themselves don't even know and so, rather than take a chance lending money to individuals or to one another, their reaction has been to hoard their cash.

One bank that swung for the fences by gorging on a boatload of leverage and ended up choking on it was Royal Bank of Scotland (RBS). In one bold move, it acquired the Dutch banking giant ABN Amro (ABN) in October 2007 for €71 billion, or a little more than US$100 billion. In winning the bid, RBS managed to best a competing offer from Barclays, which was willing to pony up only €67.5 billion (about US$95 billion) for ABN.[2] If RBS had stayed solvent and waited a little more than a year, its $100 billion investment could have bought it all—Barclays, Citibank, Deutsche Bank, Goldman Sachs, Merrill Lynch and Morgan Stanley—and it would still have had $8 billion left over.[3]

THE THUNDERING HERD

No company epitomized the excesses of the last seven years more than Merrill Lynch. The biggest game going during the 2000s was to structure complex financial products linked to residential mortgages. And nowhere did it take on more gargantuan proportions than at Mother Merrill. To keep feeding the bonus pool, earnings had to keep crashing in. That meant hiring plenty of rainmakers: investment banking talent that could scoop up the business and help make the numbers, quarter after quarter. At Merrill Lynch, one of their big gunslingers was Christopher Ricciardi, dubbed the godfather of collateralized debt obligations (CDOs), who was brought in to make Merrill a significant *player* in this new world of structured finance.

Long considered the last-to-the-trough in securing choice investment banking assignments, Merrill Lynch was the red-headed stepchild of Wall Street, at least until recently. Big, slow and stuffed full of sixteen thousand retail brokers, Merrill was often there to take the fall for a mess that others created. But that began to change in 1997, when Stan O'Neil became the co-head of its institutional business. Under O'Neil, Merrill changed the focus of its business from placing trades for clients to trading for its own account. In 1998, O'Neil became the company's chief financial officer and in December 2002, its chief executive officer. Under O'Neil's watch, Merrill decided to juice its returns by trading in some of the most toxic mortgage-backed securities.

The person most responsible for driving Merrill's push into structuring and trading of toxic mortgage-backed securities was Ricciardi. For a while, the firm prospered. In 2003, Merrill was responsible for originating just $1.3 billion of these securities; by 2006, it led the league tables with underwritings of $44 billion.[4] For his troubles, Ricciardi was well compensated. According to the *Wall Street Journal*, Ricciardi received a pay package of $8 million in 2006, before he jumped ship to a client firm of Merrill's.[5]

In 2006 and 2007, Merrill Lynch decided to increase its exposure to these exotic securities, even though interest rates were moving higher—a signal the good times might be ending. So addicted had Merrill become to the fee income from underwriting these securities that it took the unbelievable step of bringing a boatload of them onto its balance sheet. "The amounts were staggering," says Scott Sprinzen, an analyst with Standard & Poor's.[6] In effect, Merrill was acting as both an agent and a principal in a whole range of transactions. But with O'Neil at the helm, and fees ranging between 1.5 and 1.75 per cent of the total underwriting, there was no backing down for Merrill.[7] In 2006, *Fortune* magazine reported that Merrill earned up to $700 million in financing CDOs, most of them linked to subprime mortgages. According to Bloomberg, a news and information service, Merrill and Citigroup collectively sold nearly a third of the $72 billion worth of CDOs issued in 2005.[8] The reason for this push into less-transparent products was simple—money. For selling a typical investment-grade bond, the most an investment bank would hope to earn is 0.4 per cent of the total underwriting. With CDOs and similar products, they could earn three times that amount.

But the chickens were coming home to roost. The wizards of Wall Street, like drug pushers, had been abusing too many of their own products for too long. By the time the predictable began to happen, they had become addicted to easy money and lavish living. The products that Merrill and others had shovelled out the door to get their next fix started blowing up. Lending money to people who couldn't afford to pay you back turned out to be a poor idea after all. Complicating matters was the fact that the default rate on the mortgages that backstopped many of the structures Merrill had sold started to soar. In October 2007, Merrill Lynch announced a writedown of $7.9 billion associated with subprime loans. But the problem was worse than it originally appeared. Merrill's total exposure to subprime paper was estimated to be $41 billion against an equity base of just $38 billion. If the market got wind of this situation, Merrill would be toast.

By late October 2007, Merrill's board had had enough of Stan O'Neil and his push into subprime-related products. They demanded his resignation. But O'Neil didn't go away empty-handed. Reports have surfaced that his total severance package was as high as $161.5 million.[9]

HEADS I WIN, TAILS YOU LOSE

The compensation model on Wall Street is a simple one: pay for individual performance. In reality, however, the true risk taker is *you*, the unsuspecting member of the investing public. Public ownership of investment banks and commercial banks allowed these firms to grow large and profitable. But in the end, that profitability was really a mirage. The truly profitable business was taking in deposits and lending out money—not a very sexy business model, but stable and profitable. What the Wall Street wizards were *really* good at was *gaming* the situation. After all, they had control over the financial models that determined how profitable a deal was and, by extension, how big their pay was. Management didn't care what their models were spewing out as long as they were getting rich, or, as some have suggested, the "organizational scope" was just too great for them to get a handle on the situation. And investors didn't ask tough questions until it was too late. With the real risk transferred to the shareholders of the firm, the inmates had free run of the asylum.

Like Enron, Wall Street found that doing plain vanilla deals wasn't all that exciting. The secret was to find the next great thing, ride it until it crashed and, with any luck, be off making tons of money doing something else by the time the smoke cleared. This time round, there were no winners. The game Wall Street created went out with one giant bang. For those at the top it was sweet; for everyone else it was tragic.

WALL STREET FLATLINES

On Sunday, September 14, 2008, Lehman Brothers, the fourth-largest investment bank in the U.S., filed for bankruptcy protection. The bank, founded in 1850, had grown to become one of the largest dealers and investors in securities linked to the U.S. subprime market. A week before filing for bankruptcy protection, the firm reported the largest writedown in its history—a $7.8 billion loss. The meltdown of Wall Street had begun in earnest. In the three weeks following the Lehman bankruptcy filing, the S&P 500 Index shed 12.3 per cent and the S&P/TSX Index shed 15.3 per cent. Seemingly overnight, the centre of economic influence in the U.S. migrated from Wall Street to Constitution Avenue in Washington—headquarters of the U.S. Federal Reserve.

But the drama didn't stop there. On September 21, 2008, the two most storied names on Wall Street—Goldman Sachs and Morgan Stanley—received approval from the board of governors of the U.S. Federal Reserve to become bank holding companies. With their stocks under intense pressure, a conversion from pure play investment banks to bank holding companies would give these two access to the financial resources of the Fed. They desperately needed a change in status to avoid imminent bankruptcy. The end of Wall Street had finally arrived.

EMERGENCY SURGERY

Normally, the Fed's job is to establish monetary policy for the nation. By establishing a benchmark short-term interest rate, the Fed is able to slow economic growth (by raising the benchmark rate) or stimulate economic activity (by lowering it). But in times of economic distress, the Fed acts as the lender of last resort, to ensure the smooth functioning of the U.S. financial system. After the terrorist attacks of 9/11, the Fed announced in a press release: "The Federal Reserve System is open and operating. The discount window is available to meet liquidity needs."[10] With the U.S. financial system facing a crisis of confidence that could lead, if left unchecked, to a complete collapse of the entire U.S. banking sector, the Fed and the Department of Treasury were pressed into over-drive. The U.S. financial system *could not* be allowed to fail.

In case after case, the U.S. Fed and the Department of the Treasury have performed emergency surgery just to keep their patients alive. The conservatorship of Freddie Mac and Fannie Mae, arranging the marriage of Bear Stearns and JPMorgan Chase, bailing out AIG and supporting the commercial paper market kept the lights on into the wee hours of the morning in Washington. While in many of these cases the U.S. government issued a guarantee, rather than a direct outlay of cash, such as the increased limits on federal deposit insurance, the amounts that the U.S. government has spent or pledged are neverthe-less truly staggering. During the fall of 2008, the balance sheet of the Fed *doubled*—a telltale sign that the U.S. government was increasing the currency supply by literally printing money to honour its debts.

By intervening in the market to save the banks, the Fed and Treasury made the significant ideological step of converting—overnight—U.S. free-market capitalist enterprises to socialist institutions. Senator Jim Bunning of Kentucky had this to say when he learned that Freddie Mac and Fannie Mae had entered into a government conservatorship: "When I picked up my newspaper yesterday, I thought that I woke up in France. It turns out socialism is alive and well in America."[11] The tally so far on this little shopping spree by the Fed and the U.S. Treasury is an unbelievable $15 trillion and climbing—an amount greater than the entirety of America's 2008 gross domestic product.

GOING GLOBAL?

The crisis has not only dealt Wall Street a death blow but left much of Western Europe a shambles as well. Already, analysts are raising red flags about the ability of various international governments to raise enough debt capital to fund the bailouts of their banks. The *Financial Times* reported that Roger Brown, head of rates research at the invest-ment bank UBS, had voiced concern that there may not be enough investor appetite to buy up a planned issuance of $2.535 trillion in new debt in 2009.[12] Global finance has become so tenuous that during the fall of 2008, insurance premiums (credit default swaps or CDS) on non-payment of debt are higher for the debt issued by the government of the United Kingdom than that of HSBC, a London-based global bank.[13]

OH CANADA

Too small? Too uncompetitive to compete globally? When it comes to a national dialogue on bank mergers, we've heard it all before. Yet in an international sea of red ink, Canada's banks are a relative oasis of calm. Not to say that we don't have our own issues with asset-backed commercial paper, but we managed to avoid most of the *really bad* stuff. And that puts Canada's banks in an enviable position globally, one that will allow us to steal market share when the rest of the world is mopping up its financial services sector for years to come. For five consecutive years, RBC Capital Markets has been a top-ranked under-writer of bonds and equities in Canada and is one of a precious few banks globally to still retain a triple A credit rating. Another Canadian bank on the move is TD Financial. Ed Clark, CEO of TD Financial Group, put it this way: "There isn't anyone in New York that we can't at least talk to about a role at TD. We've never, ever, been in a position like this."[14]

For Canadian banks, it's this simple: do what you love, without the pressure to pull a rabbit out of the hat each and every quarter. Our banks are better capitalized and offer a more balanced business model, and while results matter they aren't the only thing that matters. In the U.S., those at the top of the financial institutions found that the lavish pay could not be beat, but for many middle- and senior-level people, the tremendous personal and family stress brought about by the win-ner-take-all culture of Wall Street was a killer. Wall Street's loss will be Canada's gain, as talented Americans opt to become a little more Canadian in their approach to the business of banking.

DOING IT RIGHT

We Canadians have been called too conservative, even by ourselves. We are—but isn't that a *good* thing? While the Royal Bank of Scotland (RBS) was lapping up perfumed mortgage-backed securities and gobbling up market share, our banks were staying put. Today, RBS is owned by the U.K. government. By missing the boat on the subprime mortgage mess, our banks now have some of the highest capital ratios in the world. Foreign banks have repeatedly gone to their host governments begging for handouts, while our banks have been able to raise the necessary capital in the Canadian equity and debt markets. This is a market where the strong will get stronger; the companies whose balance sheets aren't impaired, and who don't rely on their host governments for bailouts with strings attached, are the financial institutions that will thrive going forward. Canada's banks are the ones in the driver's seat for the opportunities that lie ahead.

What cratered Wall Street and many of the major money-centre banks globally was excessive leverage. They owed too much and owned too little. In Europe, the situation was worse. The amount of leverage at some of the largest European financial institutions got as high as a jaw-dropping 60 to 1. Leverage during the good times can help a firm magnify its profits, but when the inevitable downturn occurs the losses are also magnified. In an interconnected and wired world, both good news and bad news travel *fast*. The leverage that banks had so recklessly used to goose their earnings and bonuses in the good times turned out to be incendiary in the bad times. When shareholders sold en masse, governments around the globe had no choice but to step in and save the day. The alternative would have been too great for elected politicians to bear.

But in the aftermath of the financial crisis, it became abundantly clear that Canada had escaped the meltdown largely unscathed. As figure 4.1 illustrates, the reason was obvious. Canadian banks never leveraged themselves to the hilt in the pursuit of shorter-term financial gains. Canada's cautious nature had prevailed, leaving our banks still standing on their own after the collapse.

FIGURE 4.1 If You Play with Fire You Might Get Burned!

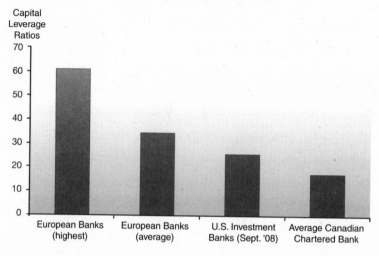

Source: CIBC World Markets

Fund managers from around the world are waking up and realizing that they need more exposure to Canadian banks in their investment portfolios. After all, Canada boasts two of only four triple-A rated banks in the world. And that has Canadian bank analysts racking up all kinds of air miles—flying to London, New York and Boston to tell the story of Canada and its banks.

GLOBAL BANKER

Canada's banking system is *the* global market model of the future. Unlike the American system, where nearly ten thousand banks are spread throughout the country, our six major banks are truly national in scope, something that allows regional differences to be exploited to the banks' advantage. A slowdown in eastern Canada, for example, might be offset by strength in western Canada. Moreover, we have a multi-pronged approach to banking: a solid retail branch network augmented with brokerage, asset management and wholesale (investment banking) operations. It's a model that JPMorgan Chase and Bank of America—two of the surviving banks from the Wall Street massacre—have adopted as the ticket to long-term viability.

Regulatory oversight is another area where Canada scores high marks. After attending the G20 meeting in San Paulo, Brazil, in November 2008, Bank of Canada governor Mark Carney said, "There are elements of the Canadian regulatory regime...that are being given serious consideration in terms of a new global capital standard."[15] Weakened competition, strong regulatory oversight and a leading-edge business model have all coalesced to make Canada the envy of the global banking world.

Our banks enjoy strong brand recognition, which allows them to grow without taking on unnecessary risks. According to *Canadian Business* magazine, the big five chartered banks and Manulife Financial count among the top eight brands in Canada.[16] The largest asset manager in the country is RBC Financial Group and the most successful and largest credit card issuers are TD, Royal and CIBC. In the U.S., the largest credit card issuers are Bank of America, Citigroup and JPMorgan Chase, which account for more than half of the cards in circulation. But with the U.S. banking sector consolidating and with continued weakness forecast for U.S. consumers and businesses, a massive contraction in credit is being forecast for the American economy. Meredith Whitney is an analyst who, while at Oppenheimer & Co. in New York, went on record in December 2008 warning that the U.S. credit card industry may pull back more than $2 trillion in credit lines from consumers by the end of 2009 alone.[17]

By contrast, over the last ten years, Canadian banks have shown a compounded annual growth rate of 10 per cent for their dividends and 40 per cent for earnings growth—an impressive feat. With a strong domestic base of retail depositors, and U.S. competitors in retreat, this could be a golden opportunity for Canada to extend its global reach in banking by acquiring U.S. and international banks on the cheap.

HOG TOWN WORLD HEADQUARTERS?

Toronto, the third-largest financial services centre in North America after New York and Chicago, could be a huge beneficiary of the financial crisis if Mayor David Miller and others have their way. According to the September 2008 issue of the Global Financial Centres Index, Toronto now ranks twelfth in the world of global financial capitals, putting it ahead of cities like Paris, Dublin and San Francisco, and the possibility of Toronto breaking into the top ten global financial services centres by leapfrogging over established players such as Boston, Frankfurt and Chicago is very real, given the relative calm of our markets in the wake of this disaster. With Toronto's financial services sector contributing more than $9 billion of tax revenues to government coffers and supporting one out of three downtown lawyers and accountants, politicians are all ears. Mayor Miller recently allocated $10 million to establish Invest Toronto, an agency dedicated to helping Toronto become a top ten global financial services centre.

Janet Ecker, a former finance minister and now president of Toronto Financial Services Alliance, an industry think-tank focused on expanding the scope and reach of Bay Street, believes that if Bay Street can bankroll the city and province, then perhaps it can bring those skills to the world. Among the initiatives that the group is working on is making Toronto the world headquarters for a new international securities regulator. If that were to succeed, Toronto would become a key meeting place for the world's finance ministers, central bankers and financial elite.

The Toronto Stock Exchange (TSX) is already taking its show on the road, aggressively trying to recruit American and foreign listings to the exchange. In 2007, the TSX conducted a ten-city road tour throughout the U.S. to showcase Toronto as an alternative place for companies to publicly list themselves. And the TSX has plenty to toot its horn about: it lists more than four thousand companies—more than any other exchange (with the exception of Mumbai) as well as more energy and mining companies than any other exchange. In technology, the TSX has the second-largest number of listings globally after the NASDAQ. Because of the relatively small size of the Canadian economy, the TSX specializes in smaller-capitalization companies, making it a perfect exchange for mid-sized U.S. and global firms.[18]

The financial meltdown has made it clear that Toronto is a city on the move, while New York may be stuck in neutral for a while. And with almost three hundred thousand people employed in the financial services sector, Canada's largest city is ideally placed in terms of its culture, education and geography to capitalize on its new role. It also has the second-largest society of Chartered Financial Analysts (CFAs)—holders of the global gold standard in financial education—in the world. Toronto-bashing may be a national pastime in Canada, but with its core cadre of highly educated professionals, a large stock exchange and the strongest banking sector in the Organisation of Economic Co-operation and Development (OECD), it is in a unique position to benefit from the financial follies of the other global financial services centres.

INSURE THIS

Canadian life insurance companies have had their struggles lately, but compared with their American peers, our companies, like our banks, are in an enviable position. Manulife had issues with its segregated funds in the fall of 2008, but emerged from the struggle to become the biggest insurance company in North America. The Putnam Investments subsidiary at Great-West Life has been disappointing, but its problems pale in comparison with what is happening south of the border.

Since many American insurance companies were also active participants in the market for side bets that the wizards of Wall Street created, the U.S. life insurance universe has literally been decimated. Insurance companies around the world rely on the stock market for funding their future liabilities, making their stock price far more tied to the overall health of the stock market than is the case for banks. Faced with these headwinds, the U.S. life insurance industry is trading at a 60 to 87 per cent discount from its 2007 levels, making it a very attractive acquisition target to better capitalized and better operated Canadian life insurance companies.

WHEN TO WADE IN

The Canadian banks have been a mainstay of investors' portfolios over the years, and once this crisis ends, they will become an even more important and integral part of them again. Their global dominance will increase and their profitability will remain strong. Rather than facing years of painful restructuring, the Canadian banks have a once-in-a-lifetime opportunity to become significant global players in retail and investment banking.

Your signal to increase your portfolio weighting toward the Canadian banks will be when U.S. residential real estate prices stop falling and when the KBW Bank Index (NYSE: BKX) outperforms the S&P 500 Index for at least two months. Real estate is the collateral behind these problem-plagued loans and it must stop falling before the U.S. banks will have a hope of recovering. The Canadian banks, while in a good position, will not recover as long as the U.S. banks are still falling. Research from RBC shows that since the 1940s, in virtually every case when the economy was in a recession and the stock market was in bear-market territory, it was the banks that led the way toward an eventual bull market.

The earnings of life insurance companies are much more sensitive to the fluctuations in the stock market than are the banks. Once the banks stage a recovery, it will be safe for investors to venture back into Canadian life insurance companies again.

CHAPTER SUMMARY

- The U.S. is spending trillions to bail out its floundering banks.
- The U.S. dollar will weaken against the Canadian dollar.
- Canadian banks, with their sound fundamentals, are poised to become significant global competitors.
- Banks, followed by insurance companies, typically lead a stock market recovery.
- Buy the banks once U.S. real estate prices stop falling and the KBW Bank Index has outperformed the broader market for at least two months.

5

BLING: INVESTING IN GOLD

Colourful promoters, dazzling investment scams and overnight riches are all part of gold's rich and sometimes scandalous history. In Canada, investing in gold still conjures up bad memories of the notorious Bre-X scandal. Few subjects polarize the investment community to the same degree. For some, it is a barbarous relic; for others, it is the second coming. Views on gold are as varied as the coveted jewellery it produces. These factors, combined with gold's emotional lure, put this precious metal in an asset class all by itself.

The current global financial crisis, with its epicentre in the U.S., is set to create a perfect storm for gold, which often outperforms stocks, bonds and real estate during times of economic unrest. The investment record is clear: gold zigs when the U.S. dollar zags. With the U.S. Fed pumping billions into the market and the lowest ratio *ever* of gold to dollars, the price of gold will rise higher and Canada—home to companies that produce more than 30 per cent of the world's gold—will be a huge beneficiary of the fallout from New York and Washington. What's more, the Toronto Stock Exchange is *the* global leader in mining stocks, and will be the best place to invest and prosper from the unfolding crisis. Investors can profit by picking up shares in gold-producing companies, gold mutual funds and exchange traded funds (ETFs) linked to the performance of gold.

HAIL MARY

In mid-December 2008, in a bold effort to resuscitate the ailing American economy, the U.S. Fed slashed its benchmark federal funds rate to near zero. So dire was the economic situation in Washington and New York that the Fed had little choice but to attempt the financial equivalent of a Hail Mary pass. With the prospect of deflation looming and massive job losses on the not too distant horizon, the governors of the Fed did more than chop the benchmark rate to almost nil; they also pledged to "employ all available tools to promote the resumption of sustainable economic growth."[1]

With its options running out, the U.S. Fed is increasingly looking at more innovative ways to try to stimulate economic growth. If rock bottom interest rates don't put people in a spending and lending mood, then perhaps the Fed can buy up lots of mortgages to drive interest rates lower—or so the thinking goes. The size of the Fed's balance sheet doubled over the course of 2008 as it sopped up the mess from a U.S. financial system run amok. But that is only the start of America's problems, because the overall level of government indebtedness is set to rise sharply as this crisis continues to play itself out. For the final two months of 2008, the U.S. federal deficit was $401.6 billion, just shy of the $455 billion it posted for *all* of 2007. And that may be the *good* news. Merrill Lynch economist David Rosenberg projects that the 2009 federal deficit could actually top $1.5 trillion,[2] if the various stimulus packages that Congress is mulling over are as large as expected.

So far, U.S. officials have focused on stimulating economic growth and warding off the ravages of deflation. But at what cost?

Already, short-term interest rates are near zero on government debt, and long-term interest rates on thirty-year U.S. government debt are yielding less than 3 per cent. Until now, nervous investors have been content to park their money in U.S. treasuries, figuring it's better to accept a lousy return than risk losing their money altogether. But with the U.S. financial condition continuing to deteriorate, the question is whether global investors will continue to buy American bonds. Already, many are balking. Low yields on U.S. treasuries and deteriorating fundamentals for the American economy make a slide in the U.S. dollar look likely. That's bad news for America, but good news for gold and the Canadian giants that mine the metal around the globe.

THE BOGEYMAN OF JAPAN

Like America, Japan more than a decade ago experienced a massive run-up in real estate and stocks that ended in a crash. While the Bank of Japan intervened early by slashing interest rates, prices for real estate and stocks continued to tumble, leaving Japan in a low-growth, low-interest rate, deflationary trap that has lasted for more than fifteen years. The very real prospect that America could be the next Japan is no doubt keeping many U.S. officials up at night.

For decades, Japan had it great. Americans fretted as Japanese companies went on a buying spree, acquiring national treasures such as California's Pebble Beach golf course and the Rockefeller Center in New York. In cars, cameras and televisions, Japan's economy was on the move, quickly becoming the second-largest in the world. But the good times couldn't last. With low interest rates making lots of cheap money readily available, Japanese companies bought up all the property and stocks they could get their hands on, pushing prices into the stratosphere along the way. When the party abruptly ended, the Bank of Japan slashed interest rates and felt obliged to prop up failed banks.

Unfortunately for Japan, the results have been disappointing. The country has seen a decline in average prices of about 1 per cent a year, resulting in rising unemployment, slow growth and intractable problems in the financial and banking sectors. Today, sluggish economic growth and a low interest rate environment have forced most Japanese investors to search for a decent yield outside of their country. Japanese house prices are down 40 per cent from their bubble era highs and the stock market is less than one-fifth its 1989 peak.

Deflation, or falling prices, is a very dangerous condition for an economy. When prices are falling, consumers have no incentive to spend, since prices will always be lower tomorrow. Buying dwindles as consumers wait for prices to drop or to firm up. In such a situation, suppliers have little choice but to continue to slash prices in the hope of attracting consumers. Deflationary environments also cause investors to go on strike as stock prices and earnings come under pressure and business and personal borrowing slumps with the rising cost of taking out loans. In short, prices fall, investment and consumption slow and growth falls when deflation rears its ugly head.

Back in 2002, the question of whether the U.S. could end up in the same predicament as Japan was put to Ben Bernanke, the current chairman of the Fed, when he was still a Fed governor. His answer was "the U.S. government has a technology, called a printing press (or, today, its electronic equivalent), that allows it to produce as many U.S. dollars as it wishes at essentially no cost."[3] The game plan of the Fed is simple: slash short-term interest rates to zero and then devalue the currency to stimulate demand. It's a formula that sets the stage perfectly for a rise in the price of gold.

RULE BRITANNIA

With the Fed ready, willing and able to turn on the printing presses to stop a wave of deflation from washing up on America's shores, a decline in the U.S. dollar seems inevitable. Some argue that the dollar's status as the reserve currency of the world will help to keep it from falling despite the actions of the Fed and Congress. It's an argument that would seem to hold some water, given that the U.S. dollar is used as the basis for pricing internationally traded commodities such as oil and gold. Unfortunately, the history of the world's reserve currencies reveals a different story.

During the nineteenth century, London, rather than New York, was the financial capital of the world and most commodities were priced in pounds sterling. Britain's pre-eminence as a trading nation and its strong network of colonies helped propel London and the pound to global dominance. During that time, Britain was the world's largest creditor nation, as well as the leading exporter of manufactured goods and services. So dominant was Britain in trade and commerce that from 1860 to 1914, some 60 per cent of global trade was invoiced and settled in pounds.

With the outbreak of the First World War, demands on the British Treasury became intense. As a result, in 1914 Britain switched from being a net creditor nation to a net debtor nation and became beholden to the rest of the world to fund its economy. The Second World War further depleted the British Treasury and Britain was forced to liquidate most of its international currency holdings to satisfy its war debts. By 1945, the U.S. dollar had replaced the pound sterling as the world's reserve currency and the pound began to decline in value. In 1956, a run on the pound caused the currency to collapse and forced the British government to seek a financial bailout from the International Monetary Fund.

Some have argued that there is no alternative to the U.S. dollar as the reserve currency of the world, backstopping global trade. But that flies in the face of the historic reality of reserve currencies. The U.K. was once the dominant military superpower and economic engine of the world. But the cost of funding its empire and staggering war debts led to a collapse in the pound and a surrendering of global economic leadership. The current levels of U.S. government debt are without historic precedent, a fact that makes a fall in the U.S. dollar a virtual certainty. The euro or, perhaps in time, the Chinese renminbi (people's currency) could one day challenge the U.S. dollar for world reserve currency status. What is clear is that currencies rise and fall on the basis of their economic health. And while that may be bad news for the dollar, it's good news for gold, which historically has moved in the opposite direction to the value of the U.S. dollar.

FIGURE 5.1 Gold Zigs When the U.S. Dollar Zags

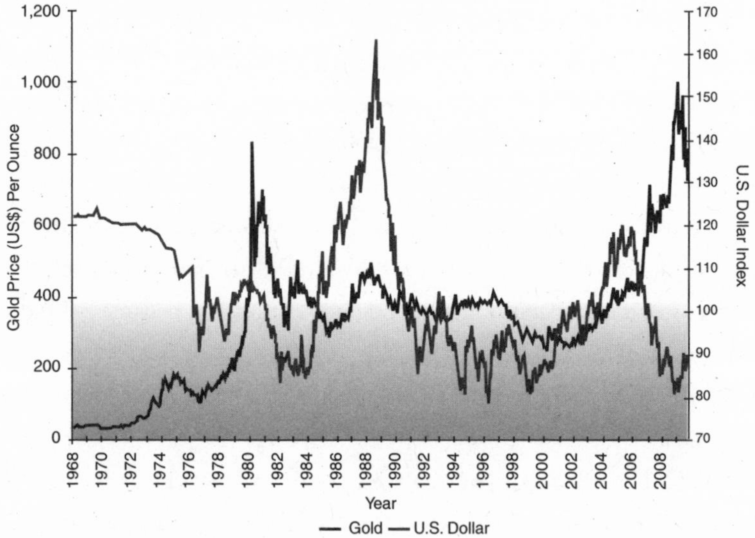

A STORE OF VALUE

Because only a finite supply of gold is available in the world, it's a commodity that holds its value over time. From the beginning of time, gold has been prized for its lustre and rarity. So rare is gold that only 161,000 tonnes of it have ever been pulled from the earth's surface—an amount that would fill just two Olympic-sized swimming pools.[4] And while more than half the world's gold has been produced in the last fifty years, easy-to-find gold is a thing of the past. Today, large mining companies, as well as millions of artisanal miners worldwide, are engaged in the hunt for gold. More than 250 tons of rock must be removed to find enough gold for a single wedding ring, an undertaking that makes gold mining the most waste intensive of all mining operations.[5]

PAPER PROMISES

The supply and circulation of U.S. dollars is tightly controlled by the Fed through its monetary policies. Unfortunately, central banks—the Fed being no exception—have a pretty poor track record of defending the value of their currencies. When push comes to shove, most central bankers are all too happy to print money and flood the financial system with increasingly worthless dollars, yen or Deutschmarks to pay off their country's debts.

Germany is a case in point. From 1914 to 1923, the German central bank printed enormous quantities of German mark banknotes to help finance the war, debasing the currency in the process. To avoid a run on the nation's gold reserves, convertibility of the German mark into gold was suspended, with disastrous consequences for ordinary citizens. Stuck with near-worthless banknotes, Germans had to resort to carting around wheelbarrows of currency to pay for everyday items. By the end of the war, the amount of money in circulation increased fourfold and hyperinflation set in. So much money was in circulation that citizens lost faith in the value of paper money, resulting in constantly increasing prices for goods. By late 1923, the Weimar Republic was issuing postage stamps with a face value of 50 billion marks and 1 U.S. dollar was equivalent to 1 trillion marks, the monetary system of Germany had been effectively destroyed.

GOLD AS CURRENCY

Investors flock to gold in uncertain times, reassured, perhaps, by its status as a one-time currency and a crucial backstop to the world's financial system. Today, gold bullion trades on the currency desks, rather than the commodity desks, at the world's major investment banks and brokerages, suggesting that it is still viewed—at least by professional traders—as an alternative form of currency.

From 1880 to 1914 and again in the period 1946 to 1971, the global economy operated under a system known as the gold standard. Under this standard, countries agreed to exchange their currencies at a specified fixed ratio to an ounce of gold. In 1990, the ratio was firmly established and the U.S. government agreed to back the dollar with gold at an exchange rate of $20.67 for each ounce of gold.

But by the 1930s, the Great Depression had left America's finances in sorry shape as it struggled to cope with enormous debts. The solution to America's indebtedness seemed obvious: deflate the dollar and pay off the government's obligations. But there was a problem—the U.S. was on the gold standard, which required it to shore up the U.S. dollar with at least a 40 per cent gold backing. The American government realized that if its citizens caught wind of its scheme to print massive quantities of dollars, there would soon be lineups to convert dollars into gold, thus further depleting the government's stockpile. That put the American government between a rock and a hard place.

The solution to the dilemma came quickly. Claiming a "national emergency," President Franklin D. Roosevelt signed Presidential Executive Order 6102 in April 1933, which halted the convertibility of gold and made it illegal for U.S. citizens to hold gold coin, gold bullion or gold certificates. In effect, the order allowed the U.S. government to debase the dollar against gold to address the financial crisis stemming from the Great Depression. American citizens were forced, under threat of fines or imprisonment, to exchange their gold holdings for deflated dollars.

From 1946 to 1971, the world was once again on the gold standard. This time round, however, the U.S. government was prepared to exchange foreign holdings of U.S. dollars for gold at the rate of $35 an ounce—a premium of more than 50 per cent above prevailing market rates. It was a bonanza for foreign governments, which rushed to cash in their dollar holdings by demanding payment in gold. In 1971, with American gold stockpiles plunging, Nixon finally decided to renege on the U.S. government's pledge to convert dollars into gold. Two years later, the gold standard was abolished, allowing the U.S. dollar to be freely convertible. By 1974, gold responded by trading up sharply to an average price of $159.26 an ounce.

Today, most global currencies float freely, but from time to time there is renewed interest in returning to the gold standard. The reason for this is simple. Since the signatories to the gold standard agreed that gold could be converted freely into non-gold money, the amount of paper money in circulation at any one time would be limited by the amount of physical gold available, thus making it impossible for authorities to manipulate the currency supply by printing tons of paper money.

SUPPLY AND DEMAND FOR GOLD

Unlike most commodities, the pricing of gold doesn't strictly follow the laws of supply and demand. Its role as a former currency and the widely held perception that gold is a safe haven are far bigger determinants of gold's value in the marketplace. Today, the ratio of physical gold to currencies is at an *all-time low*, suggesting that the price of gold will move sharply higher and stay there longer than most people suspect.

In the world of global gold production, Canada is at the top of the heap. While Canada ranks far behind South Africa, China and Australia in ounces produced, it is nevertheless home to the largest gold-producing companies in the world. Canadian listed mining companies account for more than 30 per cent of all mine production, making Canada the global leader in all things golden.

Far and away the biggest driver of gold demand is its use in jewellery, which alone accounts for 66 per cent of the total. But when you tally up retail buying of exchange traded funds, as well as coins and bar hoarding, the percentage of total demand that is retail driven soars to almost 87 per cent.

Throughout Asia, gold is viewed as a status symbol and jewellery is a must-have item. Nowhere is demand for gold stronger than in India, where gold jewellery is the centrepiece of gift giving during the festival season and is also used to support an informal credit system, since it can't be debased by government and can be converted to cash quickly. With India's rapid economic growth, the country literally has experienced a gold rush. So much so that, from 2000 to 2007, Indian demand for gold accounted for one ounce out of every nine sold worldwide. Retail demand from India and China results in strong seasonal patterns for gold prices, which rally in the late summer and fall, when the Indian festival season starts and the holiday season in the West approaches.

Gold captures the imagination like few other commodities can, possessing an "attractive, visceral lure dating back to ancient times," according to Trevor Turnbull, a precious metals analyst with Scotia Capital. Egyptian hieroglyphs dating from as early as 2600 BC indicate that gold may have been the first metal used for ornamentation purposes. Companies and individuals will go to unbelievable ends to produce and hoard gold. I once toured a gold mining project in northern Quebec, where the company was in the process of moving part of an entire town so it could mine for gold. When the world is turned upside down, everybody is suddenly bullish on gold and its value shoots through the roof. Mining companies of all stripes are suddenly gold miners too and people prophesy that gold can only go higher.

But in the long run, gold prices cannot become too divorced from the realities of supply and demand. And that presents problems for gold as a longer-term investment since virtually all the gold ever mined is still around in one form or another. Gold has the weakest fundamentals of any metal. Global mine supply clocks in at around 2,600 tonnes a year but demand is around 3,600 tonnes—and the difference between the two is made up by central bank selling and the smelting of scrap gold. Not that closing the gap is a problem, since more than sixty times the amount of global annual production is stored in above-ground stocks in either central bank vaults or hoarded by individual collectors.[6]

When the time is right, small fortunes can be made by investing in the stocks of gold-producing companies. The tiny size of the market is one reason investment in gold-producing companies is so very attractive. The market capitalization of global gold equities is only around $225 billion—an amount that may seem large, until one compares it to the market capitalization of a company like Microsoft, at $255 billion, or ExxonMobil, at a staggering $403 billion. Once word gets out that gold stocks are where it's at, the crashing herd of buyers will take gold producers on a joyride skyward.

Propelled by concerns over the terrorist attacks of 9/11 and concerns about the possibility of recession, gold has already begun its long, upward march. From January 2001 to December 2008, it moved from $270 an ounce to $870 an ounce—a gain of more than 220 per cent. With a torrent of bad economic news still to come, gold should continue on this rising trajectory as officials grapple with a limited set of options to deal with the global financial crisis.

For most investors, the simplest and most direct way to add a little bling to their investment portfolio is to buy an ETF. Buying gold coins, bars or jewellery entails the constant hassle of trying to determine authenticity and purity, not to mention the problem of storage. With an ETF, however, you effectively have a percentage ownership in a physical stockpile of gold without the difficulty of having to store the gold yourself. Investing in ETFs is as easy as buying and selling a stock, and the management fees charged on ETFs are low—typically 0.4 per cent or so.

Of course, a direct investment in gold bars, jewellery or gold-linked ETFs pays no dividends or interest. Nor do most gold-mining companies, making an investment in gold a bet on the direction of the U.S.

dollar and a proxy for financial and economic uncertainty. While a small investment in gold makes sense for most portfolios, its real value is as a hedge for when the world starts to go to hell in a handcart. Today, for better or worse, is one of those times when an investment in gold is a must-have for most portfolios.

GAME PLAN

Gold is about to have its day in the sun. With our friends in Washington in full-fledged bailout mode, the printing presses will be humming away on Pennsylvania Avenue and that means one thing: the U.S. dollar is going lower and gold is going higher. That's a boon for Canadian investors and for our multinational gold-producing companies, and it's the reason I have exposure to gold and gold producers in my own portfolio. The Toronto Stock Exchange is *the* dominant market for raising capital for global gold-mining projects. While the stock exchanges in London, South Africa and Australia do raise equity capital for companies producing locally, global players wanting to raise big money come to Toronto. The biggest gold producer in the world is, in fact, Toronto-based Barrick Gold Corporation, which grew to global dominance on the back of a string of successful acquisitions and its success with the Goldstrike property in Nevada.[7]

The portfolio benefits of gold stem from the fact that the performance of the commodity is not linked to the overall direction of either the market or the economy, making a small investment in gold a savvy way to benefit from the ongoing financial crisis while chopping overall risk.

The difficulties in Washington and New York are likely to persist for some time and, as long as they do, gold will outperform most other investments, allowing investors to profit from the U.S. dollar's inevitable decline. But investors also need to realize that once the U.S. dollar starts to stabilize, their honeymoon with gold will be over. In the meantime, investors can buckle up and enjoy the ride.

CHAPTER SUMMARY

- Gold pays no dividends or interest, but provides reduced risk and enhanced return to a diversified portfolio.
- When the U.S. dollar is weak, inflation is on the rise and banks are in trouble, gold is a good place to be.
- The best way to get exposure to gold is through an exchange traded fund (ETF).
- Even if the rest of the stock market is in the tank, gold and gold-producing companies can outperform other investments.

6

HOT HOUSING: INVESTING IN REAL ESTATE

The housing market in Canada, so recently on fire, has cooled. Consumer confidence has slumped along with house prices. In the United States, the market has imploded, sending homeowners, real estate agents and bankers scurrying for cover. With our major trading partner in full-blown crisis mode and a significant proportion of our wealth tied up in real estate, Canadians are asking, *Will we suffer the same fate?*

We won't. A slowing economy, softening commodity prices and slumping consumer confidence will continue to depress real estate prices further in most Canadian markets. But even with housing prices dropping, Canada's more conservative lending practices and relative absence of speculative activity will spare our market from a major collapse.

Real estate prices in the U.S. have tumbled hard—down 31 per cent* from their 2006 peak—and they could decline an additional 15 per cent before all is said and done. Aggressive lending practices, securitization of mortgages and a complete lack of credit standards helped propel American home prices into the stratosphere and will make their crash deeper and longer than the downturn in our housing market.

In Canada, rising employment levels, soaring commodity prices, a healthy stock market and a favourable demographic trend propelled the real estate market, but it never experienced the same frothiness as the U.S. Our market declined 11 per cent from 2007 to 2008 and a further correction is coming, yet many of the problems that turned the U.S. into the Wild West of mortgage lending never occurred in Canada. House prices in Canada are expected to slide further, but the fall will be less dramatic and our recovery quicker than in the States.

SAFE AS HOUSES

In Canada, banks and trust companies generate and hold the vast majority of the mortgages on their books. This greatly curbed the potential for the really aggressive lending practices that occurred in the U.S. Since banks in Canada, for the most part, are stuck holding the mortgages they sell, they have a vested interest in enforcing higher appraisal standards and eliminating aggressive mortgage origination practices such as the no-income-no-job-no-assets (NINJA) loans that flourished south of the border. Securitization of mortgages was a non-event in Canada, with only 24 per cent of mortgages taken "off balance sheet" and turned into securitized products.[1] The vast majority of the mortgage securitizations done in Canada were through Canada Mortgage and Housing Corporation (CMHC), a Crown corporation that carries the explicit backing of the government of Canada.

---

*As measured by the Case-Shiller Home Price Index; the peak prices in U.S. real estate occurred in the second quarter of 2006.

Our more stable banking sector, with its less predatory approach, helped prevent a massive bubble from forming around Canadian real estate. Investment bank Goldman Sachs has noticed the attractive fundamentals of the Canadian economy, particularly our banking system, which "appears to be in relatively good shape, in comparison with the rest of the G10," in the words of a recent research report.[2]

Canada has managed to avoid the worst of U.S.-style lending practices, but, starting in 2006, we quietly left the front door open for American lenders, such as AIG, to waltz in and start offering no-money-down and forty-year mortgages to Canadians. In May of that year, the Conservative government tabled a budget that for the first time allowed private insurers to come to Canada. In announcing these changes to our mortgage market, Finance Minister Jim Flaherty proclaimed that they would "result in greater choice and innovation in the market for mortgage insurance, benefitting customers and promoting home ownership."[3]

For decades, Canada's mortgage market was a dull, staid business, dominated by the hulking presence of CMHC and its smaller competitor—Genworth Mortgage Insurance Co., a division of General Electric. Armed with federal government guarantees, these two companies had free rein in Canada's lucrative mortgage insurance market. The large size and high fee structure of Canada's market have long been the envy of American competitors. Homebuyers shy of the 20 per cent minimum down payment on a home were required by law to get mortgage insurance. In exchange for fat premiums, CMHC or Genworth bore the risk in case buyers defaulted. But with Flaherty's new budget, not only were restrictions reduced, but Ottawa now was prepared to guarantee the business of U.S. insurers and raise the total federal guarantee to $200 billion. The result was predictable. First AIG, then Triad Guarantee Inc. of North Carolina, arrived in Canada. From 2006 to 2008, borrowing for forty-year amortizing mortgages grew from zero to $56 billion.

With new players tumbling into our mortgage market and offering more *flexible* products, the riskiness in the U.S. mortgage market quickly spread across the border and infected ours. In response to competitive pressures from the new U.S. entrants, stodgy CMHC announced that it would offer interest-only mortgages as well as "insurance for mortgages with longer amortizations and more flexible repayment options."[4] In October 2006, Genworth upped the ante again and started offering forty-year mortgage insurance.[5] Surprisingly, CMHC was quick to follow suit and within a month started offering forty-year mortgages and insurance on mortgages that covered 100 per cent of home prices.[6] Some had speculated that the next "innovation" to wash up on our shores would be a fifty-year mortgage. The moves did not go unnoticed by David Dodge, a former governor of the Bank of Canada. In October 2006, *CBC News* reported that Dodge had written to CMHC expressing his view that extending loans and insuring interest-only loans were "very unhelpful" and were likely to drive up house prices for Canadians.[7]

While there were warning signs that Canada's mortgage market might be overheating, the federal government was content to have a "wait and see" attitude to the rising risk in the sector. In July 2008, after repeated warnings from a wide variety of experts, the government finally acted to bring order to the market by fixing the maximum amortization period at thirty-five years and requiring a 5 per cent down payment for any government-backed mortgage.[8] But as the global financial crisis spread, concern only increased that Canada's brief experiment with higher-risk lending practices might not have been such a good idea. In December 2008, the Bank of Canada once again sounded the alarm that there were a number of "vulnerable households" that could face crushing debts as job losses spread and many people were unable to pay their bills.[9] The central bank went on to say that the 3 per cent of households in Canada with a debt-to-income ratio above 40 per cent could double by the end of 2009 if the crisis continued unabated.

Products such as the forty-year mortgages and no-money-down mortgages did their part to distort house pricing in Canada, but compared with the U.S., our foray into high-risk lending was really pretty benign. Unlike the U.S. market, where 20 to 25 per cent of new mortgages were subprime, Canada's lending to more questionable creditworthy customers was limited to 5 to 6 per cent of outstanding mortgages.[10]

TIME BOMB

While Canada had a brief flirtation with risky mortgages, the U.S. had a full-blown love affair with them. But for all the turmoil in the American housing market, the worst may lie ahead. The ticking time bomb that could plunge U.S. housing prices even lower are option adjustable rate mortgages (option ARMs), whose promise—cutting homeowners' existing mortgage payments in half—was irresistible to millions of Americans.

Option ARMs made buying a home a reality for practically everyone, even when common sense should have made it clear that the deal was too good to be true. In the process, these products helped prolong the U.S. housing boom, particularly in the hottest housing markets, for much longer than should ever have been the case. Baffling jargon and a multitude of options left buyers confused about what they were signing up for. Buried in the fine print was a dirty little secret: these mortgages would reset to higher interest rates—*much* higher rates than conventional mortgages—in the very near future. In the same way that credit card companies lure you into switching to their card with a low introductory teaser rate, option ARMs seduced both existing and prospective homeowners in search of an immediate fix. In the end, option ARMs might have been the most deadly mortgage product unleashed on American homebuyers.

Option ARMs were a trap. At the end of a typically five-year introductory period, the mortgage was designed to reset to cover its full cost. And with house prices falling, rising home equity values wouldn't bail consumers out of making an already bad situation much worse. The vast majority of these mortgages have yet to reset, with Fitch Ratings expecting that at least $29 billion worth will reset in 2009 and $67 billion worth in 2010. Some experts believe that the resetting process will leave some beleaguered homeowners looking at monthly payment increases of 63 per cent or more.[11]

Prospective homeowners, caught up in the mania that surrounded rising house prices, failed to ask the critical questions and slick sales practices discouraged them from doing so. Later, as house prices soared and low teaser rate ARMs got too pricey, banks started hawking interest-only mortgages. With the contracts being sold as *affordability mortgages*, was it any wonder that prospective buyers were stepping right up to get into the home of their dreams? But even more insidious was the fact that brokers were paid *more* to sell option ARMs than they were paid to sell other mortgage products. As a result, the product flew off the shelves as borrowers lapped up $389 billion worth of option ARMs in 2004 and 2005.[12]

The *Globe and Mail* cited the example of a couple who found in 2008 that the monthly payments on the house in Stockton, California, they had bought four years earlier had doubled. When they purchased the $425,000 house, the couple took out an interest-only mortgage. When the monthly payments reset, they skyrocketed to a little more than $4,000 a month. The pair aren't sure they'll be able to make the payments. Making matters worse—the house has tumbled in value and is now worth just $240,000.[13]

BUY AND HOLD

Canadian cities are losing some of their economic momentum, but their slide should be modest compared with the pratfall happening in the U.S. In the last six months of 2008, cities in western Canada saw the biggest loss of economic momentum since the beginning of 2008 and are at risk of further weakness in the housing market.[14] According to Derek Holt, a vice-president at Scotia Capital Economics, expectations are for house prices in Canada to decline another 10 to 15 per cent in 2009. Nor will the pain be shared equally among the various regions of the country. Oil-rich Alberta, where Holt expects house prices could tumble an additional 25 per cent by 2010, will feel the pinch more than most.

The West saw the biggest run-up in prices in the country as the commodity boom made Alberta *the* destination for young professionals from 2000 to 2007. As crude oil surged from $32 a barrel in December 2003 to a peak of more than $147 a barrel in July 2008, workers flocked to Alberta in search of work. House prices rose in lockstep with soaring commodity prices. Alberta's economy also benefited from the lowest marginal tax rate in the country, with top wage earners taxed at 39 per cent, a figure far below the 53 per cent paid by Quebeckers.[15] Across Canada, the average resale home price in November 2008 was $280,880, down from the peak pricing in May 2008 of $316,896.[16] Vancouver has the highest average housing price in Canada ($535,598 in September 2008—down from $582,354 a year earlier) for a couple of obvious reasons: it is a world-class city that boasts a wonderful setting and is Canada's gateway to the booming markets in Asia.[17] Strong metal prices, bustling commerce and net migration from the rest of Canada and abroad helped send Vancouver real estate to stratospheric heights over the past ten years.

But for now, the bloom is off the rose in western Canada, as commodity prices and a slumping economy have depressed house prices. In West Vancouver, an upscale suburb, house prices fell 22 per cent between October 2007 and November 2008. *Bloomberg News* cites the example of Sean Hanley, a West Vancouver builder, who thought that Canada's real estate market would be immune from the recession that caused U.S. house prices to tumble. After his 6,000-square-foot home had been on the market for a year, Hanley decided to chop the asking price from $4.3 million to $3.99 million and to offer a $100,000 bonus on top of the regular real estate fees to the agent who brings him a qualified buyer.[18]

Regina and Saskatoon, on the other hand, have seen very strong real estate markets—a situation likely to continue. Saskatchewan has experienced strong migration from other provinces as people have flocked there for opportunities in the oil and gas industry as well as in the fertilizer business. According to CIBC World Markets, Regina and Saskatoon rank first and third, respectively, in terms of economic momentum nationally.[19] Strong population growth, the best pace of job creation in the country and a below-average rate of personal and corporate bankruptcy are some of the reasons Saskatchewan has come out on top.

WHAT GOES UP

Canadian real estate prices will probably slump another 10 to 15 per cent on average and begin to trough in early 2010. The markets of Calgary and Edmonton will drop more than that, with the current trend of buyers driving the bus on residential pricing continuing unabated until 2010. Vancouver's market should follow a pattern similar to that in Alberta, with double-digit declines in prices over the next year. By property type (single family versus multi-unit residential), housing in Vancouver, Canada's priciest city, was roughly double the national average cost in mid-2008.

While Montreal's market is more affordable than most, a softening labour market and above-average numbers of corporate and personal bankruptcies will keep a lid on pricing for quite a while. Saint John, New Brunswick, and Halifax were hot markets through much of 2008. But while their growth rates will slow and then dip, the better affordability of the markets out East and the region's appealing lifestyle should keep house prices from plunging.

With the North American car industry in free-fall, the Ontario cities of Windsor and Oshawa will see sharp price drops in their housing, with little, if any, chance of recovery any time in the near future. Central Canada's manufacturing sector lost 400,000 jobs from 2003 to 2008, a figure that is sure to go higher as car plants, auto parts manufacturers and car dealerships fold up shop and as car sales dwindle. Windsor, the city with the highest unemployment levels in Canada, will be hit especially hard. In August 2008, Windsor's unemployment rate stood at 9.6 per cent and, with more auto sector job losses looming, real estate prices in this city are due to enter a prolonged slump.[20]

GO WEST, YOUNG MAN

Canadian real estate may be down, but it certainly isn't out. With its strong banking sector, lack of subprime problems and relatively modest run-up, Canada is poised to enter the recovery ward in 2010. According to an April 2008 study by the International Monetary Fund, Canada and Austria are the two countries where real estate prices are most justified by the fundamentals in the marketplace. According to the study, the countries that experienced the largest unexplained increases in house prices were Ireland, the Netherlands and the United Kingdom.[21] Not surprisingly, these are countries whose banking systems were the most leveraged and where conservative lending practices weren't followed.

BRICKS AND MORTAR

When global economic growth resumes and commodity prices rebound, the West will once again be best. In Alberta, low tax rates and strong commodity prices will continue to see the province grow in population and importance within Canada. In 2010, Vancouver also should see its real estate market bottom and then head higher as the Olympic Winter Games shine a spotlight on the West and its appealing lifestyle.

Prospective homeowners may want to take advantage of the downturn in the market to make the move out West. But while house prices in the West will stage the biggest recovery, the strong upward price momentum that we saw from 1997 to 2007 in residential real estate will not be repeated. Scotia Capital's Holt believes that "long-term price appreciation in real estate should move in line with inflation and population growth." Canadian real estate saw a dramatic rise in value from the beginning of 1998 to the end of 2007, averaging an increase of 8 per cent a year, a phenomenon unlikely to be repeated for quite some time.[22] Canadians should expect instead more modest growth rates across the country, the West being a notable exception. Real estate prices will probably start moving higher in 2010, but with growth rates at a more realistic 3 to 4 per cent.

Slower growth rates in the future will continue to shift the balance of power toward the homebuyer and away from the seller. Multiple offers above the asking price and offers submitted without conditions are likely to be a thing of the past. With prices declining, current homeowners should stay put if they can. According to Amy Williamson, a real estate agent with Bosley Real Estate in Toronto, in late 2008 buyers seemed to be waiting to make purchases, believing prices hadn't yet hit bottom. With buyers on strike and sales volumes contracting, many sellers are becoming more realistic about their asking prices, and bidding wars, once common, are becoming rare.[23] Bottoming interest rates could make late 2009 or early 2010 a good time to consider refinancing an existing mortgage. Interest rates will stay low for some time, so the decision on whether to lock in a long-term, fixed-rate mortgage or go with a floating-rate mortgage depends on how much you have to finance. While floating-rate products typically save money in the long run, a surprise jump in rates can leave homeowners stressed.

Housing traditionally has been considered a great investment because of its tendency to keep pace with inflation as well as population growth—that and the fact that it is a leveraged investment—but that doesn't make it perfect. With interest rates down and employment prospects dimming, homeowners who find they have bitten off more than they can chew with their mortgage should certainly try to reduce their monthly carrying costs by paying it down as fast as possible. Another smart strategy is to increase the value of your home by taking advantage of the greater availability and lower cost of labour by undertaking a modest home renovation. The projects with the highest returns on investment are interior painting, kitchens and bathrooms.[24] Unless you think the economy is going to collapse completely and there will be no economic growth whatsoever—an unlikely scenario—owning your own home makes great sense.

With house prices coming off the boil nationwide, renting for a year or two longer waiting for interest rates to bottom out would be a smart strategy for potential first-time homeowners. Across the country, the rental market has been tightening up, with the average vacancy rate for rental accommodation standing at 2.2 per cent in October 2008. Calgary tops the list of most expensive cities in Canada in which to rent, according to a study by CMHC, with the average two-bedroom apartment setting you back $1,148 per month. The cheapest place in the country to put down stakes is Sherbrooke, Quebec, where the average rental cost for a two-bedroom apartment was just $543 a month.[25]

A LEVERAGED BET

Investors love real estate. It offers steady, stable returns linked to inflation and local market conditions. But what investors *really* like about real estate is the chance to buy a property for a modest amount of money down while borrowing big. Find a tenant or two to carry your costs and presto, you've got yourself a great investment. But with the world's financial system on the operating table, banks and trust companies are calling in their loans, and investors and speculators who thought real estate prices would go up forever are stuck trying to sell properties in a market that has turned cold.

Luckily for Canada, our quiet, steady ways kept real estate speculators at bay and will make our real estate bust relatively mild on a global scale. According to research by RBC, investor-owned mortgages accounted for a paltry 2 per cent of the total market in Canada.[26] In the United States and the United Kingdom, investors accounted for 10 per cent of outstanding mortgages.

Condominiums are the one segment of the Canadian real estate market where a speculative bubble has formed. While most of our home mortgages are held by end users, data from Clayton Research, a leading Canadian real estate firm, shows that as many as 40 per cent of condominium mortgages are held for investment purposes. In the major urban centres, condominium construction is the mainstay of new home building. In Toronto, condominium construction accounted for 50 per cent of all new construction and in Vancouver it accounted for 50 to 60 per cent.[27] According to William Tharp, a senior economist with Dundee Securities, "Condominiums are just more subject to speculative activity, with much bigger price swings than single family homes." Lower entry price points, small initial deposits on new builds and the opportunity to lease or sell property on closing have all helped encourage speculation in the condominium market, and prices are likely to drop much faster and stay depressed for longer than in any other segment of the real estate market.[28]

But not all condominiums are created equal. Williamson believes it's possible to determine where the real value in condo properties is. "Condos with terraces, parking spots and multiple bedrooms draw purchases from end-users rather than speculators. Larger buildings stuffed full of smaller one-bedroom units tend to attract more speculative activity," she says.

One area of the market that is looking very attractive is real estate investment trusts (REITs). REITs, which are professionally managed and trade on the Toronto Stock Exchange alongside other stocks, offer investors relatively stable yields and the potential for price appreciation. REITs are publicly listed securities that allow investors to own a fractional share of an operating business. In the case of REITs, the operating business is the ownership, development and management of commercial properties. The professional managers of a REIT collect fees and rents from their tenants, passing most of the money through to the investors in the REIT. Rather than trying to pocket a little extra cash by renting out a basement apartment in their home, investors can invest in a REIT and scoop a little cash without getting their hands dirty. The sector is broken down into a variety of sub-categories, with individual REITs specializing in owning and operating hotels, seniors' residences, apartments, office buildings and shopping centres. The sector has been badly beaten up with the implosion of the global banks and with the ensuing panic in the stock market; however, distribution yields across the sector in 2008 averaged a healthy 12 per cent. Real estate and REIT analyst Karine MacIndoe of BMO Capital Markets thinks REITs look attractive, but she urges caution. Her approach in these tougher markets is to play great defence and look to buy a position in the REITs that specialize in the apartment sector, seniors' housing and "basic needs" retail. While it looks probable that yields will fall as various REITs cut distribution, even if they were to fall into the 7 to 8 per cent range, they would still present an unusually good buying opportunity for investors.

CHAPTER SUMMARY

- Canadian house prices will continue to slump but will not hit the lows experienced in the U.S.
- The fundamentals for Canadian real estate are among the best in the world.
- Prices will trough around 2010, then start to rebound.
- Buyers should tread cautiously in the condo market, where the biggest speculative bubble has formed.
- REITs are a great way to get more exposure to real estate without the headaches of ownership.

7

A BRIDGE TOO FAR: INFRASTRUCTURE INVESTING

With America and much of the world gripped in the jaws of a major recession, governments are stepping in with enormous so-called stimulus packages to get people working. But rather than slashing taxes and hoping citizens will spend the savings at the mall, governments from Brussels to Washington are targeting infrastructure spending as a way of jump-starting the economy. Roads, rails and runways are where the action is going to be over the next decade as governments try to shore up the home front. Pension funds have been drawn to the sector because returns on infrastructure investments don't correlate well with those of stocks and bonds, thus helping them to increase their overall return while slicing risk. But retail investors can also benefit from the flood of institutional dollars headed infrastructure's way. And Canada, with its ample supply of engineering talent, hydroelectricity and natural resources, will be front and centre in this emerging bull market.

THE OPEN ROAD

Infrastructure is more than "feel good" government spending—it's the critical backbone of commerce for any modern nation. Insufficient capacity at the ports can leave farm exports rotting on the dock. Traffic congestion is worse than an inconvenience: in a world where time is money, delays on American roads cost at least $78 billion annually from 2.9 billion gallons of wasted fuel and 4.2 billion lost work-related hours.[1] Flight delays in U.S. airports have cost America $15 billion each year in lost productivity.[2] Electricity shortages can bring manufacturing to a grinding halt. Having trouble making an outbound phone call because cellular networks are a little spotty? Then good luck trying to operate a call centre or other service-oriented business. Transportation and electric utilities, as well as communication and energy delivery systems, are the lifeblood of business, which means that North America's crumbling infrastructure is a big threat to our economic health.

Massive underinvestment in infrastructure over the last fifty years has left North America competitively weakened and has imperiled lives. In Canada, most of our infrastructure was built during the boom years following the Second World War—and it shows. In the fall of 2006, three lanes of an overpass on Boulevard de la Concorde in Laval, Quebec, gave way suddenly and without warning, causing the death of five people, three of whom were from the same family.[3] In Minneapolis, during the summer of 2007, the evening rush hour commute was interrupted when the entire span of the Interstate 35W Bridge collapsed, sending sixty people to hospital and killing twelve; a freight train passing underneath the bridge at the time of the collapse was cut in half by falling cars, concrete and twisted metal.[4] A 2001 report by the American Society of Civil Engineers assigned an average grade of D+ (poor) to America's stock of infrastructure.[5] According to the Federal Highway Administration, 72,000 U.S. bridges are "structurally deficient."[6] The U.S. Department of Transportation Financing

Commission was even more blunt in its 2008 assessment of America's roads, declaring the nation's surface transportation to be "in a physical and financial crisis."[7]

Decades of underinvestment in infrastructure coupled with a public demand that governments get people working with shovel-ready infrastructure projects has created a golden opportunity for this sector. The total value of current infrastructure investment globally has been pegged at $17 trillion by the World Bank, although that figure likely understates the reality because it excludes the cost of ports, oil and gas infrastructure, and airports.[8] But today, the tables have turned as citizens continue to demand action on the economic front. Annually, China is planning to spend $200 billion, Europe will spend $300 billion and the U.S. $150 billion. One-third of the global spending will be directed toward power systems and a further 40 per cent will go toward transportation infrastructure. All told, the world economy will see between $25 trillion and $30 trillion of new infrastructure spending between now and 2020.

The immense cost of major projects, coupled with changing and growing population patterns, has left North America with a significant infrastructure deficit. America has a great legacy of major infrastructure undertakings, yet the U.S. federal government has been without a development strategy for more than fifty years, its last great commitment being the creation of the interstate highway system in 1956. Infrastructure investment has lagged in North America, in part because of a culture that values self-reliance. Less than 5 per cent of Americans use public transportation to get to work, preferring instead to drive. Commercial airlines transported over 712 million passengers in 2006, whereas Amtrak, the national railway company, carried just 25 million. In Europe, it's the opposite, with the public relying far more on mass transit than private vehicles. This "do it yourself" attitude is also reflected in the fact that the U.S. spends just 2.4 per cent of its GDP on infrastructure, compared with 3 per cent in Canada, 5 per cent in

Europe and 9 per cent in China. In 2005, the American Society of Civil Engineers estimated that it would take $1.6 trillion over a five-year period to fix America's crumbling infrastructure.[9]

The United Nations expects the global population to soar from 6.6 billion to 8.3 billion by 2030, with more than 60 per cent living in urban areas. This will create enormous demands for transportation, power generation, water and sanitary systems, all of which points to an inevitable rise in infrastructure spending by government and private corporations in the years to come.

WHEN YOU'RE IN A HOLE, DO YOU KEEP DIGGING?

Faced with soaring unemployment, a dysfunctional banking sector and a supersized trade deficit, America is sprinting toward the biggest public works spending program since the creation of the interstate highway system. Describing the economic situation as "dire" and in need of "urgent and immediate action," President Barack Obama is readying lawmakers for a wave of government spending on infrastructure-related projects that could last for years. He has already unveiled a $775 billion plan to try to stimulate the U.S. economy and get Americans back to work.

The approach adopted by the Obama administration is one embraced by economists and union leaders alike. According to Terrence O'Sullivan, president of the Laborers' International Union of North America representing 500,000 construction workers, each $1 billion spent on infrastructure development creates 47,500 jobs; these are jobs in sectors such as construction, manufacturing and logistics as well as complex engineering and architectural work. Obama's plan calls for major spending on traditional road-building projects and on "green" and new technologies to help boost long-term competitiveness.[10] Under the plan, Obama envisions millions of such green jobs in the solar and wind power sectors, although just how he plans to create them still remains to be seen.

In the United States, there is more than $136 billion in infrastructure projects that could get people back to work between now and 2011. In Canada, we have at least $14 billion worth of projects lined up for 2009 alone. Unlike a lot of government undertakings, infrastructure spending actually has a multiplier effect that is nothing to sneeze at. CIBC World Markets estimates, for example, that in the U.S. a 1 per cent increase in infrastructure spending has twice the economic benefit of a tax cut of the same dollar amount.[11]

When the world economy begins to grow again, infrastructure will remain critical to supporting economic growth. American ports are presently operating at approximately 90 per cent capacity and CIBC World Markets has reported that surging world trade could double the demands on them by 2020. Since 1988, American roads have seen a near doubling of vehicle miles travelled despite only a 1 per cent increase in highway mileage.[12]

FORGET THE SLOW BOAT TO CHINA—WE'LL DRIVE

Like the U.S., China has responded to the global financial crisis with its own $586 billion economic stimulus package geared toward infrastructure spending through 2010, which—at 15 per cent of GDP—will help accelerate the country's build-out of roads, railways and airports and serve as an accelerant for the building boom already underway. Remarkably, a little more than a decade ago China had few, if any, highways. Yet today it has completed almost 43,000 miles, an amount equivalent to America's entire interstate network. China's current five-year plan aimed at massive modernization will also quadruple investment in the country's railways. Projects are already underway to link Shanghai, the nation's business capital, with Beijing by high-speed train. In addition, Beijing recently completed a major extension of its subway system, expanding from 114 kilometres of track to 540 in little more than a decade. China's ports, already in the top nine of the fifty largest in the world, are also developing, with planned spending of $50 billion by 2012. So enormous is the ongoing infrastructure program in China that it eclipses the efforts of the Marshall Plan, which was designed to rebuild Europe after the Second World War.[13]

At the other end of the spectrum is India, a country where infrastructure is sorely lacking. Highways are responsible for transporting 70 per cent of all goods within the country yet they amount to only 2 per cent of all roads.[14] Ninety per cent of passengers travel by road in India, despite the fact that they are often narrow, with buses, trucks, rickshaws and occasionally pedestrians jockeying with cars for space. There are fewer than 6,400 kilometres of interstate-calibre highways, a full one-third of which are just single lane. What's more, India's infrastructure is creaking at a time when annual sales of passenger vehicles are set to double to 2 million cars a year by 2010. The poor quality of the roads, combined with an influx of new, poorly trained drivers, resulted in more than a hundred thousand traffic fatalities in 2007—one of the worst records in the world. The situation is so bad that the World Bank has estimated that traffic accidents actually shave 3 per cent off India's $1 trillion GDP.[15]

India's port system is also in need of a major overhaul, with turnaround times for cargo ships averaging three to five days, a snail-like pace compared with the five hours it typically takes in Hong Kong or Singapore. Power shortages are also common, with peak demand outstripping supply by more than 15 per cent. And power demand is set to double by 2020. Electricity transmission is poor throughout much of the country, and a full 45 per cent of Indian households are without power entirely. To address these challenges, the Indian government is embarking on a whopping $500 billion spending program over the next five years to upgrade its airports, roads and railways.

CANADA CONSTRUCTS

Canada will be one of the biggest beneficiaries of the global rush to invest in all things infrastructure. For example, Bombardier, the best manufacturer of mass transit systems in the world, is a Canadian company.

As cities around the world begin to invest in subways and commuter trains, Canadians will be there to help. If it's large-scale engineering design and construction projects that need to be completed, Canada is home to global leaders in the field. Canada has what a recovering world will need to get going again. And that will create huge demands in this country for more oil pipeline, rail lines and port capacity to satisfy the coming global hunger for our resources.

In Canada, government spending on infrastructure has tumbled over the past three decades, falling steadily to less than 4 per cent in 2007 from approximately 40 per cent of GDP during the 1960s. More than 60 per cent of our infrastructure is between 50 and 150 years old and has already reached 80 per cent of its engineered life expectancy, which means that urgent action is necessary to prevent more catastrophic failures. The Laval bridge collapse, along with the global financial crisis, has helped put infrastructure spending back on the front page of newspapers, and the Canadian government has responded in kind, earmarking a record $6 billion for infrastructure spending in 2009, most of which is targeted toward beefing up the country's roads, bridges, tunnels and public transit.[16]

While our infrastructure deficit is somewhat less daunting than America's, we still have our work cut out for us. To bring it up to par and meet anticipated future needs, Canadians will spend an estimated $300 billion between now and 2025, with almost two-thirds of this required for maintenance and updates to the country's stock of transportation and water systems.[17]

Another major development here at home has been an increased proportion of the gas tax allocated to infrastructure by municipalities. In just three years, this has increased fivefold, to 36 per cent. John Baird, Minister of Transport, Infrastructure and Communities, has promised that gas tax transfers for municipal infrastructure will rise in 2009 to $2 billion per year from $1 billion and stay at that level on a permanent basis.[18]

Beyond federal initiatives, many Canadian provinces are also beefing up infrastructure spending to remain competitive with other international jurisdictions and spur employment growth. Ontario, acting in co-operation with the U.S. Federal Highway Administration and the Government of Canada, has announced a $1.6 billion project to link Ontario's Highway 401 near Windsor to Interstate 75 in Michigan via a new international bridge. Alberta has announced an investment of $22.2 billion over three years to be spent on hospitals, roads, schools and municipalities to meet the needs of a growing economy and population.[19] Saskatchewan is planning an infrastructure spending spree of $5.5 billion between now and 2012, and British Columbia has several major initiatives underway, including its preparation for the 2010 Winter Olympics and the Sea-to-Sky Highway Improvement Project. All told, B.C. will spend about $20 billion on infrastructure projects by 2012.

BUILDING YOUR PORTFOLIO, ONE BRICK AT A TIME

Not since the era of Franklin D. Roosevelt and the New Deal—a massive series of programs aimed at getting people working during the Great Depression—has America embarked on such massive infrastructure expenditures. But this time around, America's spending is being matched around the world as nervous governments shoot the locks off their wallets in a collective effort to get their countries working again. The sooner this happens, the better off Canada and Canadian investors will be, since Canada is a key supplier to the world of the future. In the meantime, Canadian infrastructure companies will be picking up projects both here and abroad as governments step into the fray and start to spend.

In engineering expertise and construction expertise, Canada ranks among the world's best. According to a July 2008 study by *Engineering News-Record* (ENR), Canada's SNC Lavalin is the top power and water design firm in the world.[20] And with water and power ranking near the top of the infrastructure food chain, that's good news for Canada. The same is true in transportation systems where Canada is a global leader.

. Already, the orders are starting to tumble in. Bombardier is based in Montreal but is a global transportation company that employs sixty thousand people and is the third-largest civil aircraft manufacturer and the largest rail equipment manufacturer globally. It is one business that will benefit from the increased largesse of governments worldwide.[21] While many companies around the world were laying off workers and grousing about slumping sales, Bombardier posted a blockbuster third quarter in 2008—more than doubling profit from a year before. Bombardier Transportation, the company's rail division, is in a great position to win contracts for high-speed trains and subway systems as governments in Britain and China target these as key areas for infrastructure spending. All through the slump, governments have been placing orders for rail equipment, resulting in a four-year backlog for Bombardier Transportation's European division.[22]

Montreal is running out of space at its port, one of the main gateways for goods entering the U.S. Midwest and eastern Canada. In 2008, traffic was up 10.3 per cent from the year before, in part because of Montreal's position 1,600 kilometres inland, which gives it a huge leg-up on other competitors along the eastern seaboard. A manufacturer in Germany that needs to ship product to Chicago, for example, can save two days' shipping time by going through Montreal instead of New York. But the benefits don't stop there. An integrated transportation network, including one hundred kilometres of railway connecting the port's berths with the Canadian Pacific and Canadian National rail lines also help to boost the port's competitive advantage. To maintain its edge, the port of Montreal has embarked on an ambitious, $2.5 billion program called Vision 2020 that will triple the port's container capacity by that year.[23]

Hydro-Québec has had no shortage of suitors interested in its low-cost hydro electricity, and is set to cash in on the global boom in infrastructure-related spending by selling to two utilities in New England for a twenty-year term beginning in 2014. NSTAR Inc., the largest electric and gas utility in the state of Massachusetts with annual revenues of $3.3 billion, and Northeast Utilities Inc., the largest utility in New England with more than 2 million electric and natural gas customers, are currently lobbying the U.S. Federal Energy Regulatory Commission (FERC) to build a $700 million transmission line from New Hampshire to Sherbrooke, Quebec, in order to bring power to customers in New England. Currently, exports of power to the U.S. account for a disproportionate portion of Hydro-Québec's profits—a proportion that is likely to increase in the years ahead as the company signs more lucrative contracts with other utilities outside the province.[24]

THIS ROAD IS PAVED WITH GOLD

Roads, rails and runways are all the rage, but one smart way to benefit from the boom in infrastructure is by buying the stocks of engineering and construction firms that will be at its forefront. With money flowing into the sector from both private and public coffers, engineering and construction firms are on the cusp of entering into a golden era where pricing power will offset cost pressures. SNC-Lavalin, a global engineering and construction company headquartered in Montreal, should do extremely well as the infrastructure bandwagon gains momentum. Bechtel Corporation of San Francisco is another well-known company offering integrated engineering and construction services to businesses and governments globally.

Another way to profit from this megatrend is to buy an ETF that holds a basket of infrastructure-related equities, such as engineering firms, construction companies, utilities, companies selling industrial equipment and those selling building materials. While ETFs offer lots of diversity and low fees—two huge benefits for investors—most infrastructure ETFs have performed poorly over the last few years, partly because they are heavily weighted toward electric utilities, a sector less likely to benefit from infrastructure spending. The gains from such spending are more likely to be experienced by engineering and construction firms that can show an immediate pop in their bottom line once the money begins flowing.[25]

As part of a broader investment portfolio, infrastructure investments make tons of sense since their returns aren't closely related to those of stocks or bonds. As a result, they help boost portfolio returns while chopping risk. Once a dam, port, railway system or other critical piece of infrastructure gets built, it throws off cash for decades to come. Airports, toll roads and electric transmission lines all provide essential economic scaffolding, so the demand for their services should remain strong for years to come. The useful life of bridges and roadways is often fifty years or more, so once they're built, they can power your portfolio as tolls and user fees continue to roll in. Best yet, because major infrastructure projects are enormous undertakings both in terms of time and money, they often boast high margins with little, if any, competition to worry about.

The benefits of infrastructure investing have not gone unnoticed; already pension funds around the world are warming up to it. Direct investments in infrastructure assets, such as roadways and airports, help large institutional players such as pension funds achieve greater portfolio returns with less risk than an investment portfolio of just stocks and bonds. That has institutional investors licking their chops and clamouring for a piece of the infrastructure pie.

Governments will lead the initial charge into infrastructure investing with a massive increase in spending, but what will continue the investment boom for decades to come is private money that will be following in the governments' footsteps. Even modest changes in the portfolio weightings of the large pension funds can flood the sector with boatloads of cash, creating a rising tide for your investments. According to

CIBC World Markets, the largest Canadian pension funds have more than $700 billion under administration, of which 5 per cent is currently allocated to infrastructure; it estimates, however, that this will increase by anywhere from 10 to 15 per cent by 2017, adding an additional $200 billion in new money toward such projects.[26]

Investors looking to profit from the coming boom in infrastructure spending should look to pick up shares on pullbacks of the engineering design and construction firms, which will be its biggest beneficiaries. Canada's SNC-Lavalin, Bechtel and Fluor Corporation of Irving, Texas, all offer smart ways to play the global build-out on the backbone of the global economy.

CHAPTER SUMMARY

- Infrastructure spending is going prime time, with governments globally investing trillions.
- The West must deal with its crumbling infrastructure, whereas the developing world needs new transportation, water and sanitation systems, and electricity generators to support industrialization.
- High barriers to entry, plus contracted cash flows stretching for decades into the future, make an investment in infrastructure a winner.
- Infrastructure assets aren't well correlated with either stocks or bonds, which helps investors chop risk while boosting returns.
- ETFs are a smart way to get wide exposure to infrastructure, but heavy weightings toward utilities sometimes depress returns.

8

NOT A DROP TO DRINK: INVESTING IN WATER

Bridges and ports are essential for supporting commerce, but water is critical to life itself. A growing, rapidly industrializing global population and a push toward water-intensive agriculture have made water stress a fact of life for 40 per cent of the world's inhabitants. It's a situation expected to get worse, with 64 per cent of the world expected to experience water shortages by 2025.[1] Goldman Sachs estimates that global water consumption is doubling every twenty years, a rate of growth described by the investment bank as "unsustainable." Now, however, a potent combination of looming government expenditures and private investment interest is set to fill the void for the world's water needs, setting the stage for a good news story for investors.

Global water demand is growing rapidly, but water supply is relatively constant. Water evaporates from the world's oceans and lakes, which, in turn, are replenished by rainfall. The vast majority of the world's surface area (more than 70 per cent) is covered by water, but most of that is salty seawater unfit for human consumption. Fresh, potable water constitutes only 2.5 per cent of the world's total supply, of which more than 70 per cent is frozen in the icecaps of Greenland and Antarctica and therefore inaccessible to humans. Making matters worse, just nine countries account for 60 per cent of the world's available fresh water supply, Canada and Norway chief among them. These factors, combined with vastly different global consumption rates and pricing, have made water investments both critical and profitable in recent years.

Most of the current growth in water demand is from developing economies where massive urbanization is creating unprecedented need. As with all resources experiencing strong demand and sluggish supply, the price of water and the stock of companies that can effectively deliver water solutions is set to move higher. According to CIBC World Markets, from 2002 to 2005, U.S.-based water companies managed to outperform the broad S&P 500 stock index by more than three to one. And the stock performance for international water companies over the same time frame was even more spectacular, rising twice as fast as their U.S. counterparts.[2]

THE BOTTOM OF THE BUCKET

In North America, we take our easy access to clean water for granted. But water contamination and an uneven availability of water supply is contributing to high water stress through much of the developing world. According to the World Health Organization, water contamination contributes to 80 per cent of all disease and sickness globally. A shocking 1.1 billion people are without access to clean drinking water.[3] The World Bank estimates that in China, 90 per cent of the major rivers are seriously polluted and cannot support aquatic life. The annual economic cost of China's water pollution has been estimated at $21.4 billion. In 2007, poor water quality in China resulted in lost industrial production of $12 billion.[4]

In Beijing, water shortages are "set to reach crisis point" according to reports from Xinhua, China's official news agency. So bad is the problem that a 307-kilometre water pipeline was completed in September 2008 to bring water from the Wangkuai Reservoir in Hebei Province. With its reservoirs one-tenth full and two-thirds of the city's water being drawn from underground aquifers, the situation in Beijing is critical. So much water is being sucked from below ground that the water table around the city is dropping by a metre a year. The cost of diverting water from other regions in the country has been high. In the area around the Wangkuai Reservoir, farmers have gone without water for two years and a local hydroelectric plant has been idled.[5]

Tourists to China and India are often struck by the apparent lack of water in these countries. Unlike Canada, their landscapes aren't dotted with rivers, streams or lakes. Shanghai, a city of 20 million people, is surrounded by the crowded, polluted Yangtze River, where tourist boats compete with floating electronic billboards advertising a wide range of electronic products and massive cargo ships looking to re-stock at what is now the busiest port in the world. When I was there in 2007, it wasn't until the third day of my stay, when the prevailing wind changed direction and blew the smog out to sea, that I was able to view the top two-thirds of the magnificent modern buildings dotting this financial and commercial hub. Air and water pollution are two very real challenges that China will have to balance against rapid and often unrestrained economic growth.

Globally, however, the regions with the highest water stress are North Africa and the Middle East. The United Arab Emirates and Saudi Arabia suffer from the greatest water scarcity, with just 62 and 112 cubic metres per person available annually.[6] The average North American, by contrast, has a water supply per person of 28,800 cubic metres—a stunning difference of more than 257 times. To combat water shortages, the countries of the Arab Gulf have been building desalination plants to convert sea water to drinking water, the region now being home to 55 per cent of such facilities worldwide. From 2002 to 2007, global desalination capacity has increased by 47 per cent.

Water shortages and pollution are having an impact on both people's health and important industries, such as tourism, in many other parts of the world. Within Europe, evidence of chronic water shortages has shown up over the last few years in countries such as Malta, Spain and Italy, all of which have already depleted more than 20 per cent of their annual available water supply. Droughts throughout the region have only exacerbated the problem. The most striking testament to Barcelona's water shortage is the site of the eleventh-century church of Sant Roma. Since the 1960s, when the valley where the church stood was flooded to provide water to the Catalonia area, the only visible reminder of the church's existence was its bell tower peeking above the water. With a plunging water supply and persistent drought, however, it has now completely re-emerged, attracting crowds of gawking tourists eager to catch a glimpse of it and the parched water reservoir that surrounds it.

FIGURE 8.1 The Church of Sant Roma

Source: Getty Images

During the summer of 2008, Barcelona's water shortages became so chronic that local officials had no choice but to charter ships to supply drinking water to meet the needs of locals and tourists. While clearly designed as a stop-gap measure, the ships did manage to boost the city's water supply by around 6 per cent, but at an estimated cost of just under $62 million—more than half of which was spent on infrastructure for the port. Without the water shipments and an active, aggressive campaign to reduce water, the city might have to face the prospect of reduced water supply—a situation it hasn't experienced since 1953.[7]

SPRINGING A LEAK?

In North America, our water infrastructure is in urgent need of repair or replacement, with estimates for the work in the hundreds of billions of dollars.[8] According to CIBC World Markets, some of America's water systems date back to the Lincoln administration and, in some cities, half the water intended for consumers fails to reach its destination because of leaking valves and pipes. What's more, at least 20 per cent of America's municipal water systems do not comply with federal regulations. In Montreal, a major downtown intersection was closed in January 2009 when subzero conditions caused an underground main dating back to 1891 to burst.

Before a water pipeline ruptures, it leaks, and for existing water pipelines, leakage is a major concern. Water pipes can be expected to last anywhere between fifty and a hundred years, but this is highly dependent on environmental conditions. And Canada, with its harsh climate, is not particularly conducive to long-lived infrastructure assets.

Water leakage is a major consideration all over the globe. In the U.K., leakage rates have been falling, but on average they are running at 23 per cent (down from 30 per cent), meaning that of all the water that starts out at source, only 77 per cent makes it to its final destination. In the Czech Republic, the situation is worse, with only 67 per cent of the water in that country ever making it to its final destination.

MAKE THAT AN EVIAN

The increased consumption of water-intensive, protein-based foods like meat put an even greater strain on global water supply. Meat-based diets have helped people to grow larger and stronger and thus have been associated for centuries with health and affluence. Since agriculture accounts for 70 per cent of water demand globally, changing patterns of food consumption can have a dramatic impact. Raising just a single head of beef cattle takes 4,000 cubic metres of water, for example, whereas a kilogram of rice requires just 1.9 cubic metres.

The supply of clean, accessible water is also under strain because of a growing world population that is looking to emulate life in the water-rich West. The good life calls for an abundance of water—for cleaning, cooking, bathing, drinking and wasting. At fancy restaurants, bottled water from mountain springs or naturally carbonated water is the norm. In North America, bottled water is still big business, with annualized sales of approximately US$85 billion. So pervasive is water in our lives that the average American annually consumes forty times the amount of water the average African does.[9]

While we consume water like it's going out of style, personal usage pales in comparison to industry, which slurps up 22 per cent of available water for use as solvents, as raw materials or in generating steam for industrial processes. Computer chip fabrication may not seem like a water-intensive business, but it alone is believed to consume 25 per cent of Silicon Valley's fresh water. According to research from JPMorgan, the five largest food companies in the world—Anheuser-Busch, Coca-Cola, Danone, Nestlé and Unilever—consume a staggering 575 billion litres annually, enough to meet the daily requirements of everyone on the planet.[10]

QUENCHING THE THIRST

The need to replace leaky infrastructure in the West has coincided with growing water demand in the developing world, putting water investing front and centre for governments. Water prices have been surging lately, but they are anything but uniform from country to country, something partly due to the fact that water is often treated as a political tool rather than as a commodity where supply and demand are allowed to set the price. The level of subsidization, the availability of infrastructure used for transport and a region's level of agricultural intensity—all of these factors conspire to insulate us from water's true cost. Americans and Canadians have some of the lowest water costs, with the average American paying 71 per cent less than does an individual in the emerging markets and parts of Europe, according to a report by Credit Suisse.[11] The single biggest differentiator in pricing appears to be the level of subsidization, which means, not surprisingly, that many of the most heavily subsidized countries also waste the most water. It's a sad fact that, globally, 85 per cent of water that is intended for personal use is wasted.

Wide pricing differentials and huge variability from region to region in terms of water access have many people worrying about future water diversion. With U.S. rivers and aquifers starting to dry up, concern has been mounting that it's only a matter of time before Americans start eyeing our water. According to Tony Clark from the Polaris Institute, a social policy think-tank, "It is not at all clear that either Ottawa or the provinces are in a position to deal with a challenge coming from Washington to turn on the taps for Canadian bulk water exports."[12] In 1987, Environment Canada weighed in on this topic in its report *Federal Water Policy*, emphasizing the federal government's emphatic opposition to large-scale exports of our water.[13] It is clear that Ottawa is aware of the issues surrounding water exports, including the need to design appropriate policy responses in the years ahead. Others believe that, if managed correctly, this is a potential money-making opportunity for Canada.

Capitalizing on an abundance of water is easier said than done. To deliver a sufficient quantity of water to make it a viable business, a water pipeline system would need to be constructed at enormous cost.

Credit Suisse estimates that a twenty-four-inch-diameter water pipeline would cost a minimum of US$2 million per mile to build, making a long-term contract for water supply an absolute necessity before construction could begin.[14] But with water in short supply, many states may be willing to sign a twenty- or thirty-year contract to guarantee they have water when and where they need it. A water pipeline between Canada and the U.S. may be in the cards some day.

One province that is thinking of ways to exploit its strategic advantage in water is Quebec. A paper by the Montreal Economic Institute noted that if the province exported just 10 per cent of its 1 trillion cubic metres of renewable fresh water per year at a price of $0.65 per cubic metre it would generate $65 billion in gross annual income.[15] In future, the key to having our cake and eating it too will be our ability to appropriately value, regulate and price water for export. Our small population base and enviable access to water put us in a great position to capitalize on our position as water supplier to a thirsty American neighbour.

SOAKING IN THE PROFITS

The emergence of markets for traded water rights* in many of the southwestern U.S. states, as well as in Chile, Mexico and Australia, means that water may soon become a globally traded commodity like coffee or oil. If this happens, it would be priced on the basis of supply and demand, rather than some arbitrary price determined by government. With the market setting the price for water, spinoff businesses would be created to trade and hedge water-related risk in the same way that natural gas and oil contracts get traded today.

Enron was actively trying to develop water as a commodity when I worked there and had taken the first steps toward building out water

---

*The market establishes a price for water based on supply and demand in the same way that it does with oil. Currently, this market is an over-the-counter (OTC) or negotiated market and not an exchange-traded market like crude oil (NYMEX).

capabilities with its 1998 purchase of Wessex Water PLC, a U.K.-based water and sewage firm, for $2.2 billion. Had Enron succeeded, it would no doubt have manipulated a nascent water market for immense profits; however, timing is everything, and at the point when things were really turning up in the water business, Enron's stock price was turning down. With trillions of dollars of money at stake, and had outcomes been different, the company would have been rolling out water-based futures contracts—just like it did with electricity. But with government subsidies creating huge economic inefficiencies in the global water market, you can be sure that it's only a matter of time until the wizards of Wall Street find a way to start trading water futures to thirsty portfolio managers and speculators around the globe.

For now, the best way to invest in water is through the infrastructure companies that design and build dams, reservoirs and water pipelines. As it stands, the only viable way for countries or regions to manage their water deficiencies is to pump from surplus areas or to build desalination plants, and that means lots of business for companies that will be building these facilities.

Water issues may be local, but the solutions are global. Asia's unbridled urbanization and industrialization is causing widespread water and air pollution, but for investors in this sector, that's opportunity knocking. Chinese officials and the general public are all too aware of the dangers posed by rampant urbanization and are engaged in an ongoing dialogue with industry experts and researchers to take the necessary steps to reverse China's worsening environmental record. The country has already announced its willingness to have foreign companies participate in wastewater treatment and water supply projects. Companies such as SNC-Lavalin, Bechtel or Fluor, which specialize in wastewater treatment, offer ways for investors to participate in China's efforts to curb water pollution.[16]

Currently, the world has fifty-five thousand large dams and, according to the World Commission on Dams, some $2 trillion was spent on dam construction during the twentieth century. The future of dam building is in Asia, which has a significantly lower ratio of reservoir capacity to water supply compared to the United States or Europe. To increase reservoir capacity to the level present in Europe, Asia would need to see a 45 per cent increase in dams at an estimated cost of US$92 billion.[17]

The largest dam in the world is China's Three Gorges, which will be used to produce hydroelectric power from the Yangtze River. The estimated power output from the generating station is 18.2 gigawatts, or a staggering 3 per cent of China's electricity capacity. India has plans to build eighty-nine dams and hydroelectric projects to harvest the power of the fast-flowing rivers running off the Himalayan Mountains. France's Alstom is the global leader in manufacturing hydroelectric power generation equipment. The company has more than seventy-six thousand employees in seventy countries and had sales of €16.9 billion (C$27.85 billion) in 2007.

Aging infrastructure in the West, as well as the growth of desalination plants and water recycling plants worldwide, are boosting the need for spending on water pipeline and transfer solutions. China is currently developing seven major water projects, including a south-to-north water transfer project that will entail three separate routes and more than 450 kilometres of water pipelines. Seven additional large-scale water projects are also currently under consideration. In Australia, the government is examining a major pipeline network to alleviate the water deficiency in the southeast portion of the country. Australia is the driest inhabited continent and has the greatest temperature and rainfall variations anywhere in the world.

Getting direct exposure to water pipelines is best accomplished, naturally, by buying the guys who make the pipe. Northwest Pipe Company of Vancouver, Washington, is a leading supplier of large-diameter, high-pressure steel pipe products for water transmission. A rising tide of public frustration over water waste also has governments scrambling to plug the leaks. One company for investors to consider in this regard is Halma, a U.K.-based company that is the global leader in leak-detection technology.

Water investing is a great way to plug the holes in your investment portfolio. Water usage is growing at double the pace of overall world population growth as the emerging markets urbanize and farmers respond to the increasing demand for water-intensive foods. An estimated one-third of the world's population lives in countries experiencing water shortages, and in many countries water pollution is a serious issue. Water shortages can be addressed with desalination plants, dams and water transfer pipelines, but these are enormous financial and engineering undertakings. Investors looking for a flood of opportunities need to look no further than an investment in water.

CHAPTER SUMMARY

- Aging infrastructure in the West, rampant pollution in the developing world and increasing agricultural demand make water investing a smart way to benefit from rising infrastructure spending.
- Water demand is rising, but supply is relatively constant.
- Different regions within countries may have water shortages or surpluses.
- Areas with water shortages must transport it from other areas or desalinate sea water—both expensive propositions.
- Canada has one of the greatest supplies of freshwater in the world.
- To prosper in the coming bull market in water, invest in the engineering and construction firms that will build the dams and water pipelines that will be needed in the developing world.

9

GET REAL: THE CASE FOR COMMODITIES

Investors panicked as global markets tumbled throughout the fall of 2008. They pulled money out of mutual funds, hedge funds and commodities in a desperate attempt to stay afloat. Hedge funds that had borrowed heavily to magnify their gains liquidated their holdings in a hurry. One of the great ironies in this was that commodities, the best-performing asset class over the previous five years, became the *worst*-performing asset class overnight as investors sold their winners first to avoid becoming roadkill in the ensuing global margin call.

But once the market bottoms, the stocks that will rally hardest will be the oversold stocks of commodity producers, as well as financial services stocks, which were the first to fall off the table when the crisis started. When the world economy picks up, it will be the stocks levered to *global* growth rather than U.S. growth that will best the market and lift your investment portfolio higher.

NOTHING BUT THE REAL THING

So what exactly *are* commodities, anyway? They are coffee, orange juice and sugar, all probably part of your breakfast routine. They are rubber, steel and oil, which make your commute to work possible. From the time you wake up to the time you go to sleep, you are surrounded by commodities—the *real* things that you use every day.

Like stocks, commodities are traded on exchanges—futures exchanges, to be exact—and throughout the world their price levels serve as an important gauge of world industrial activity. Although important to the global economy, commodities are among the most misunderstood of all asset classes. Stocks, bonds and real estate have legions of followers and plenty of experts agree on their importance within an investment portfolio. But venture into the world of commodities and you are into a fringe area of investing where suspicions run high and understanding is limited.

Yet, despite all of the misgivings and misunderstandings, commodities are central to the value of our dollar, our way of life and the investment opportunities that we encounter as Canadians. Primary commodities, such as copper, zinc, nickel and iron ore, account for 25 per cent of global trade. In 1997 they accounted for up to 75 per cent of total exports for some of the countries in Sub-Saharan Africa, and yet commodities continue to get short shrift when it comes to the world of investing.[1]

CALLING ON COMMODITIES

As an asset class, commodities will be set to soar when global economic activity resumes and that's a huge leg-up for Canada's industries and investors. As illustrated in figure 9.1, when commodity prices are soaring, so too is our dollar. The Canadian dollar zips higher when commodities are all the rage. So what determines commodity prices? In the short run, it's demand. If demand increases, prices are sure to follow. But in the long term, supply is what drives commodity prices. And supply takes a long time to respond to an increase in demand.

FIGURE 9.1 Canada—We're Still Considered a Commodity Country

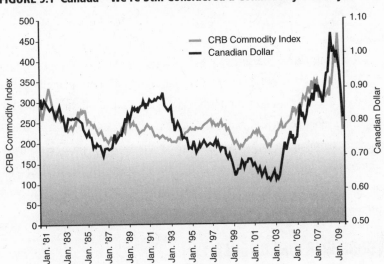

The business of commodity production is both capital and time intensive. In most cases, extensive geological studies, exploration drilling, testing and permitting are necessary before production can even begin. Once an initial deposit of oil, zinc, potash or copper is discovered, it takes anywhere from five to ten years to bring that mine or oil field into full production.

With non-governmental organizations fanning out around the world, the environment, long a hot button issue in the West, is now an important consideration globally. And that means longer, more extensive permitting requirements that push back the eventual new supply of commodities. With chronic shortages of projects, personnel and capital, strong, sustained demand very quickly translates into sharply higher prices for commodities.

The repercussions of the economic meltdown for commodity producers have been unsparing—mines have been closed, workers laid off and development for oil sands, nickel, gold and copper projects curtailed around the world. The price for energy and metals is extremely sensitive to global economic activity. Once traders and investors figured out that global economic growth would slow in the wake of a wobbling Wall Street, they sold their commodity positions, sending them into such a tailspin that the peak-to-trough decline in 2008 for the Commodity Research Bureau (CRB) index was a plunge of 55.9 per cent.

But once the crisis fades and demand begins to grow again, commodity prices will re-test the highs. With mines and oil fields in a care and maintenance mode and dispirited mining executives still shell-shocked from the depths to which their share prices plunged during the crisis, a major supply response will be a long time in coming. That sets the stage for commodity prices to move higher and *stay* higher as supply struggles in the face of newly resurgent demand.

A GOOD IDEA JUST GOT BETTER

Commodity markets still manage to confound and confuse even the experts—changing course rapidly and without warning in response to inventory reports, the weather, speculative activity and, of course, the overarching forces of supply and demand. Commodities go through long periods when prices boom and then extended periods when they bottom out. When supply is low and demand suddenly starts to shift into overdrive, you can be sure that an extended period of strong commodity prices lies ahead. According to the Yale International Center for Finance, commodity futures have been shown to offer the same returns as stocks with a similar amount of risk.[2] Better still, commodities tend to perform best when stocks and bonds are heading lower, making them a welcome addition to a well-diversified investment portfolio. The researchers in the Yale study also found that commodities provide a much better hedge against inflation, or rising prices, than either stocks or bonds. Since investors care about their real—or inflation-adjusted—purchasing power, commodities not only help diversify investment portfolios, they also help preserve wealth, since their value is tied to real assets.

In the long run, commodities help chop your overall level of risk and in the short run, strong swings in commodity prices can make you a lot of money. According to the International Monetary Fund, real returns actually fall modestly for commodities over long periods of time. Over the period from 1862 to 1999, for example, commodity prices fell a mere 1.3 per cent a year. But within that long-run trend of declining prices, there have been powerful booms in commodity prices, some lasting as long as thirty-nine years.[3] Research by *The Economist* shows that commodities follow a trend of gradual price decline over extremely long time horizons. But while there is a gradual trend toward lower prices, the historical pattern is punctuated with many multi-year periods where commodity prices have soared.

FIGURE 9.2 Economist Industrial Commodity—Price Index

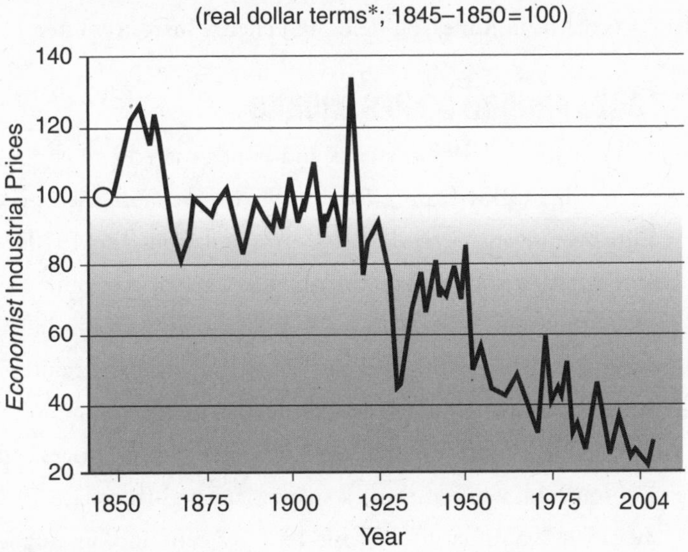

(real dollar terms*; 1845–1850=100)

Economist Industrial Prices

Source: The Economist
*Adjusted by U.S. GDP deflator

What's more, when commodities are rising and the stocks of commodity producers are doing well, you want to *buy all the Canada you can get* since our currency, stock market and many of our leading companies are tied to the fortunes of commodities. Saskatchewan is the Saudi Arabia of potash, Alberta holds the second-largest oil reserves in the world and the region around Sudbury, Ontario, is filled with rich nickel deposits, all of which will help to make Canada the epicentre of all things *real* when the global economy gets going.

Years of low commodity prices, geologists looking for other work and a lack of exploration for new resources are ultimately the factors that will sow the seeds for the next boom in commodities. I remember trying in the 1990s to recruit candidates to join Enron, then a sleepy energy company (little did they know!), when oil was trading for just $15 a barrel. It was difficult to get talented young people to join an "old economy" company when the Internet was taking off. But times change and what was once dull suddenly became dynamic as the world of commodities started to roar back to life in 2002, after twenty years of under-investment in mines, oil fields and energy infrastructure.

WHAT GOES AROUND COMES AROUND

During the 1980s and 1990s, stocks and bonds roared and commodities went nowhere. But from 1968 to 1982, it was just the opposite: commodities were on fire and so, too, was inflation. The 1970s were also a time when Europe was re-emerging as a major economic engine and Japan, Korea and Taiwan were rapidly expanding. The baby boom generation was entering the workforce and buying cars, houses and appliances, which further underpinned the demand for commodities.

After the OPEC oil embargo of 1973 took effect, oil prices spiked, increasing fourfold, while the stock market crashed from late 1973 to 1974. By 1979, U.S. inflation had hit 13.3 per cent and, in August of that year, Paul Volcker was appointed by U.S. president Jimmy Carter to serve as chairman of the Federal Reserve. Volcker got right to work, limiting growth in the money supply that had been helping to fuel inflation throughout the 1970s. By ratcheting the benchmark federal funds rate up to a high of 20 per cent in July 1981, he eventually was able to bring U.S. inflation down to 3.2 per cent by 1983—a remarkable achievement. Today, Paul Volcker is held in esteem within economic circles for conquering American stagflation during the 1970s and currently serves as the chairman of Barack Obama's economic advisory panel.

The commodity party that began in 2002, spurred on by strong demand from China and Southeast Asia, came to an abrupt halt, however, when the wheels fell off Wall Street and financing dried up for everyone. Mining and energy companies involved in bringing on massive new projects that required years of expensive development before a single tonne of concentrate or a barrel of oil could flow were suddenly cut off at the knees. Banks weren't in a position to lend, nor were investors, who had just lost their shirts in the market mayhem. And if *anyone* was going to lend or invest, it certainly wouldn't be for a prospect that wasn't going to see any production until some time in the future.

With commodity supply taking a time out, the spark of increased demand will be all that is needed to light a fire under commodity prices.

DOG EAT DOG

In declining price environments, the strong get stronger. Smart, experienced management teams know they have to anticipate an eventual pullback in the underlying commodities that they produce and they have a game plan for dealing with those circumstances. Multinational companies such as Barrick Gold Corporation and Exxon Mobil rank all their projects globally and when the going gets tough, they get going quickly—closing the money losers and transferring staff. The small, single-project companies just don't have the luxury of such options: if they shut down, they are out of business. So they continue to operate their project, until the cash or their patience runs out. But big, well-capitalized companies can use these downturns to their advantage by cherry-picking the crown jewels of their former competitors that have run into financial trouble. Pullbacks help accelerate consolidation in the industry and help increase the strength, depth and reach of the biggest and best-run companies in the industry at the expense of the start-ups.

SHANGHAI SURPRISE

Demand for commodities, when it comes, will be from the rapidly growing and expanding economies of Southeast Asia. In the decade since the Asian financial crisis, the economies of the region have undergone a complete metamorphosis, with nineteen emerging economies earning investment grade ratings on their debt—a sharp increase from ten countries just five years ago.[4] The countries of the region have massive U.S. dollar foreign currency reserves and are exporters, rather than importers, of capital. But most importantly, they are rapidly urbanizing, creating an unprecedented need for commodities. What's more, seven-eighths of the world's population lives in the developing world, suggesting that the process of industrialization will be ongoing for many years to come. In this global push to urbanize, once again it will be China driving the bus, with its total urban population expected to rise to a staggering 970 million by 2020 from 532 million in 2008.[5] That is almost six times the number of people who formed the middle class in Japan, Europe and North America from 1948 to 1963. It was also a period that corresponded, unsurprisingly, with the last great boom in mining.

DOLLAR DOLDRUMS

Underpinning the new bull market in "real" things is a weak U.S. dollar, which only is going to get weaker with the tattered state of the U.S. economy and a government bond market that is starting to resemble one of Bernie Madoff's Ponzi schemes. To pay the interest on the debt that's already been issued, America needs to find someone else to buy new debt. Likewise, to pay bondholders back when bonds mature, it needs to issue new bonds to new buyers. In other words, the whole system is dependent entirely on finding new buyers to pay off existing bondholders. But what happens when a torrent of new buyers turns into a trickle? Global investors may well get turned off by the pathetic yields they are earning on treasuries or worry, justifiably, about the prospect of the U.S. government debasing its currency to pay off its obligations. A fall in the U.S. dollar will only help to add rocket fuel to the nascent commodity boom that will be underway already in 2010. Since virtually every commodity is priced in U.S. dollars, a sharply lower dollar means higher commodity prices.

A weaker U.S. dollar, supply and demand out of whack, the renewed prospect of inflation as well as a complete and total lack of investable alternatives are the perfect storm that will help propel commodities higher. At the heart of the financial crisis was a very big lie—that house prices would continue to go up and up, forever. It was a lie so big and told so often that it will tarnish the reputation of American investment banks for years to come. Beyond reputational damage, there is also the very real damage that has been inflicted on the financial health of America's and Europe's banking sectors. Investors scrambling to make up their losses from the financial crisis of 2008 will have little patience for wading through a minefield of banks and brokers to try to find the handful of U.S. institutions that didn't stretch the truth and that have pristine financials. Why bother, when you can buy a commodity-producing company that has a solid set of financial statements and an understandable business model and offers a leveraged play on the part of the world that is rapidly urbanizing and industrializing?

AROUND THE WORLD, WITHOUT LEAVING HOME

The Toronto Stock Exchange, with its heavy emphasis on energy, materials and fertilizer stocks, will be a huge beneficiary when the world begins to grow again. Canadian investors will benefit because foreigners shopping for stocks in Canada also will be looking for commodity exposure. Rest assured that no fund manager in London, Tokyo or New York is coming to Canada to buy our banks and health care stocks. And since Canada's stock market capitalization is only 3 per cent of the total pie, Canadian investors benefit from a global pool of dollars chasing after our crown jewels. But the best part about buying Canadian commodity stocks is that it allows you to get all of the benefits of going global without the hassles of currencies, foreign accounting practices and having to become an expert in very different economies and political systems.

Over the last ten years, an investment in the Toronto Stock Exchange would have done just about as well as any of the high-flying emerging market stocks, offering all of the upside without the downside. Now that's an investment to get excited about!

FUTURE FANTASIES

One way for investors to get exposure to the fast-moving economies of Southeast Asia is to buy the underlying commodities linked to the explosive growth in the region. After all, some academic studies, such as the one at Yale, have shown that a basket of commodity futures performs better than a basket of commodity producers. The authors conclude, "Over the 41-year period between 1962 and 2003 the cumulative performance of futures has been triple the cumulative performance of 'matching' equities."[6]

But despite this evidence, there are many practical problems and perils for the amateur investor who wants to trade in commodity futures. Because they are actually contracts for the *future* delivery of commodities such as crude oil, corn, soy beans and nickel, there is always a risk that an investor won't "roll" the contract from one future time period to a later one. Failing to do so means running the risk you'll receive a phone call from a commodities broker congratulating you on becoming the proud owner of a thousand barrels of crude oil awaiting pickup in New York Harbor. While the instances of customers actually having to take unintended physical delivery is rare, trying to manage the risk associated with existing contracts when they roll into new contracts is a very real problem. Every time an investor buys an oil future, he is buying a separate contract with different pricing and time to expiry. Trust me when I say that this is a very complicated and confusing way for investors to get exposure to commodities.

The extreme volatility of commodity prices is the biggest single reason novice investors go broke. And yet it's possible to get enormous exposure to commodities with very little money down. To buy an oil future and control a thousand barrels of oil for future delivery, for instance, you need to post an initial margin of around $7,425. That means that if oil is trading for $50 a barrel, you are effectively controlling $50,000 worth (1,000 × $50/barrel) of crude oil for just $7,425. That works out to a leverage ratio of a little more than six times.

If oil pulls back sharply in a given day, the investor must post additional margin or the exchange will close out the position and debit the investor's account. A former colleague of mine once worked for Refco Futures, a one-time high-flying commodity brokerage. Back in 2005, when the commodity market was going straight up, he commented to me that his company was closing accounts faster than it was opening them. If losing your shirt seems like a good idea, then trading commodity futures may be the way for you to go.

REAL RETURNS

Confusing jargon and excessive leverage, as well as roll and currency risk, all make trading in commodities beyond the scope of all but the most seasoned of investors. There are tens of thousands of stocks to choose from, but only about fifty different traded commodities—and some only thinly so. Like smaller-capitalization stocks, these thinly traded commodities may be more subject to price manipulation and it can be difficult for an investor to exit from a big position. Not only that, but trading in commodities also means having exposure to currency risk, since most are priced in U.S. dollars.

The best way for investors to get more than enough exposure to commodities, with a lot less risk, is by buying shares in commodity-producing companies. Research from the City of London Investment Management Company Limited has shown that once a commodity bull market has been established, it is more profitable to invest in the producing companies by purchasing their stocks than by investing in the underlying commodities.* Stock ownership also offers an indirect form

---

*The City of London Investment Group is a publicly listed fund management company founded in 1991 and based in the U.K., with offices in Dubai, Singapore and the United States.

of leverage that can be very profitable to investors as the commodity bull begins to charge. While operating costs often go up in a commodity bull market, they rarely keep pace with the rate of growth in revenues and that difference means that company earnings tend to expand very dramatically. Even with increases in the commodity as modest as 20 per cent, well-operated companies can often see their earnings increase substantially *more* than 20 per cent, thereby amply rewarding shareholders for their patience.

Canada, with its financing expertise and global reputation as a resource powerhouse, is in the catbird seat to benefit from the coming commodity boom. Commodities and their producers were oversold in the market meltdown of 2008, as nervous investors sold their winning hands to avoid getting crushed by the train wreck of the global financial crisis. As a result, the stocks of the producers and the commodities themselves are now cheap—and buying value on the cheap is always a good investment strategy. Investors can participate in the inevitable growth of the developing world through the great commodity stocks that offer solid fundamentals and a leveraged bet on the future.

CHAPTER SUMMARY

- Commodities will be one of the best-performing asset classes when global growth resumes.
- Canada is ideally positioned to benefit from strong global growth in commodities.
- Commodity futures are suited only for the most seasoned investors.
- The best way to play the commodity boom is by buying shares in the producing companies.
- Commodities experience sharp bull markets followed by steep bear markets.
- Commodity returns are not well correlated to the returns of stocks or bonds, making them an effective hedge against inflation.

10

SHIFTING SANDS: INVESTING IN OIL

No other commodity is as visible, as important or as prized as oil. Access to cheap, readily available oil is more than a convenience—it is the linchpin to the world that we live in. For more than one hundred years, oil has meant power and those who control it control the lifeblood of global commerce. So important is oil to the world economy that the United States maintains the Strategic Petroleum Reserve, which holds up to 727 million barrels as a first line of defence against supply interruptions.

Concern that the Persian Gulf may some day hold the U.S. economy hostage over its dependency on oil has had many in Washington sounding alarm bells recently, but behind all the fear is the inescapable truth that Canada is *the* biggest supplier of oil to America. And with its vast energy riches, Canada is destined to become an increasingly important global supplier and, along with it, an energy superpower.

The International Energy Agency views Canada's oil sands as the single-largest source of new crude oil supply—almost three times more important to incremental global supply than Saudi Arabia. That's a boon for investors in Canada's oil sands: producers that have access to the second-largest oil reserves on the planet.

So entrenched is cheap oil to our way of thinking that the idea of going without is just too difficult to contemplate. Oil has shaped our lives—from the automobile, or two, in our driveway, to suburbia. Plastics, rubber, chemicals and even cosmetics all are made from oil, yet on a per litre basis, it costs less than orange juice. Surely, more oil will be discovered, or alternative energy will ride to the rescue, say the pundits. Yet more than one hundred years into the oil era no viable alternative has materialized. It may still happen, but I wouldn't bet on it.

ROLLER COASTER

In 2008, oil prices were down, then up sharply—and then they fell off a cliff, leaving many financial observers with a severe case of market whip-lash. On July 11, 2008, oil hit $147.27 per barrel, only to then turn back around and start plummeting downward. By December 19, 2008, it had fallen to a low of $32.40 a barrel—a decline of 78 per cent. Most people assumed the swings were due to tightening global supplies or surging demand. Few suspected that behind oil's sudden, powerful moves was another, more potent force: debt.

In good times, borrowed money can magnify investor gains. Using other people's money allows us the luxury of buying now and paying later. And if you happen to be lucky enough to buy big when interest rates are low, your carrying costs will be small.

Over the last two decades, people around the world lined up to take advantage of all those affordable mortgages that suddenly seemed to be sprouting up everywhere. After all, it made perfect sense to pile into real estate when home prices were on the rise, since a small slice of equity could be worth a whole lot more in a jiffy. Individuals bought on credit, fund companies magnified their investment gains with a healthy dollop of borrowed cash from the wizards of Wall Street and the U.S.

government helped fuel the country's growth with a heap of borrowing from foreigners.

Investors looking for a leveraged way to grab exposure to rising global growth found that oil was a great way to play it for time frames as short as six minutes or as long as six years. Oil is the most actively traded commodity market around, making it the perfect vehicle for a bet on global growth. Fund companies piled into oil futures, and so too did the wizards of Wall Street, who hired commodity specialists— many of them from Enron—to be ready for the emerging bull market in energy. Papers were written and books were published decreeing the coming shortages*; and energy prices responded to all of that invest- ment demand by moving sharply higher. In 2008, there was so much demand for crude oil futures that twenty-seven paper barrels were being traded every day on the New York Mercantile Exchange (NYMEX) for every one physical barrel consumed in the United States.[1]

With energy hitting new highs during the summer of 2008, big, leveraged bets on oil's ascent were paying off handsomely for profes- sional traders. Wall Street was making boatloads of money and so too was an aggressive new player in the financial markets: the hedge funds, which could use borrowed money from the investment banks to take enormous positions in the oil market. And the futures markets offered the hedge funds something other than just the ability to make leveraged bets; they allowed them to remain exempt from scrutiny by the U.S. Securities and Exchange Commission (SEC), the government watch- dog charged with regulating stocks and stock markets. This meant that hedge funds and investment banks were free to invest as they saw fit in the commodity markets without the prying eyes of the SEC looking into what they were doing.

It wasn't that the commodity markets in the U.S. weren't regulated at all, it was just that they were *lightly* regulated—as they were originally

---

*Energy is a generic term that often is used interchangeably with oil, but can also include natural gas and electricity as other forms of energy.

designed primarily for hedging agricultural crops. Farmers, worried about the kind of prices they were going to get for their corn crop eight months from now, could sell forward the equivalent amount of corn in the futures market and thus "lock in" the price they were going to receive. Similarly, corn oil producers or other food processing companies looking to lock in prices for their finished products could also turn to the futures markets for price stability. Commodity trading in agricultural products in the United States dates back more than 150 years, but rampant inflation during the 1970s, particularly for oil, brought it to the forefront of the investing world. In 1974, oversight of the commodity trading world became institutionalized with the formation of the Commodity Futures Trading Commission (CFTC).

ENRON ALWAYS HAD AN ANGLE

In 2000, new legislation was introduced in the U.S. Congress, heavily supported by Enron Corp., that sought to open the door to unregulated trading of financial derivatives and exempt private electronic exchanges from federal oversight. The bill was championed in the U.S. Senate by Phil Gramm, whose wife, Wendy, was then serving on the board of directors of Enron after stepping down as chairwoman of the CFTC. Enron was a major financial contributor to Mr. Gramm's campaigns and, while there is no direct evidence that he was responsible for all of the language in the bill, it was nevertheless very favourable to Enron. In December 2000, the Commodity Futures Modernization Act passed into law. During the debate, Gramm declared that the legislation, if adopted, would protect "financial markets from overregulation" and, further, that it would "position our financial services industries to be world leaders into the new century."[2] The bill contained a provision that exempted the trading in credit default swaps (CDSs)—the market for side bets that the wizards of Wall Street had created—from regulatory oversight. This, combined with its enormous leverage, allowed the CDS market to grow to enormous proportions, and, in a final twist of fate, helped to accelerate the demise of Wall Street. The bill also contained the specific language that Enron had lobbied for that would guarantee the exemption of federal oversight on electronic commodity markets.[3]

The so-called Enron Loophole was just what Enron had been seeking: unfettered access to the commodity markets in order to dominate them and manipulate prices as it saw fit. At the time, Enron had launched an electronic market of its own called Enron Online. With the passage of the bill, Enron was able to trade commodities on its own electronic exchange without worrying about federal oversight. Now that Enron had its own captive energy market, it would be in a position to drive prices up or down at will. The company's energy trading operation became so dominant that, from 2000 to 2001, it recorded almost $7 billion in profits—a mind-boggling amount even by trading standards.[4] When it collapsed, corporate records showed that Enron and other firms had used Enron Online to manipulate electricity prices in the California market, in some instances driving up prices more than 300 per cent.[5]

While Enron collapsed in December 2001, the changes it had set in motion didn't stop with its demise. Many of its most seasoned commodity traders ended up working at UBS Warburg, a Swiss investment bank that acquired Enron's trading operation after the collapse.[6] In 2003, Phil Gramm left the U.S. Senate to take up a lucrative job with UBS, where he led the charge lobbying Washington for favourable treatment for the investment banking industry on mortgage- and banking-related matters.

On July 10, 2008, the financial world was rocked when William Poole, a former president of the St. Louis Federal Reserve, declared that Fannie Mae and Freddie Mac might need a government bailout. According to Poole, "Congress ought to recognize that these firms are insolvent, that it is allowing these firms to continue to exist as bastions of privilege, financed by the taxpayer."[7] The next day, Senator Joseph Lieberman proposed legislation that would require investment banks and hedge funds to adhere to position limits in the commodity markets. Other senators, such as Carl Levin of Michigan, introduced a measure that would allow the CFTC to police individual traders in the electronic over-the-counter markets.[8] Together, the moves would effectively close the Enron Loophole. These measures were finally adopted with the passage of the U.S. Farm Bill in June 2008. Oil responded in kind by falling from more than $147 per barrel to less than $95 per barrel by the end of August 2008.

WHAT GOES UP . . .

The investment flows into the oil markets were finally dealt their death blow in the fall of 2008. On September 22, both equity and oil markets were battered when uncertainty arose around the details of the U.S. government's $700 billion Troubled Asset Relief Plan (TARP), which was intended to save the financial system. On that same day, news surfaced that Wall Street's two remaining investment banks, Goldman Sachs and Morgan Stanley, were converting to bank holding companies, which meant, in essence, that they were seeking protection from creditors through the U.S. Fed by converting from broker-dealer status to traditional banking structures.[9]

With the investment banking world in a free fall, hedge funds were also getting pummelled. Their investment portfolios were sinking and investment banks, which had previously provided credit and other forms of leverage, were yanking it away in a last-ditch effort to save themselves. All of a sudden, the massive investor demand that had helped drive oil prices skyward was reversing, and now was sending them tumbling. From September 22, 2008—when Wall Street's fate became clear—to December 19, 2008, oil fell to a low of $32.40 per barrel from approximately $120. Fund companies, investment banks and pension funds were stampeding for the exits, desperate to sell their oil futures quickly; the leverage that had helped to magnify their investment gains when oil was rising now became an accelerant magnifying their losses.

FIGURE 10.1 Oil Has Been on a Wild Ride

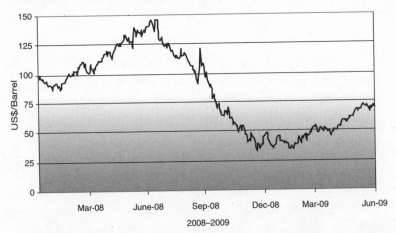

How much speculation was there in the oil market? It is a question that many have asked and few have been able to answer. My own econometric models, which analyzed such fundamental factors as global GDP, inventory levels, OPEC production, net demand and real interest rates, came up with a price of approximately $110 per barrel when oil was trading at $147 per barrel in July 2008. This suggests that there was at least $40 per barrel of speculative froth in the price of oil at the peak of the market. The upside to all this is that the stocks of oil-producing companies never reflected the highs in the oil price—the collective wisdom of the stock market may have been greater than the foolish speculation and wild gyrations of oil on the commodity markets.

With Wall Street and the hedge fund industry decimated, the likelihood of a speculative froth reappearing in the oil market any time soon is small. What's more, in their rush to exit the oil trade, the wizards and the "hedgies" sold oil and the stocks of oil-producing companies *too far*, sending their prices plunging along the way. For investors with cash, this is the time to be buying huge value on the cheap; the solid fundamentals of the oil industry still are very much intact. In other words, supply continues to struggle while demand remains strong. Once the world starts to grow again, oil and oil stocks will be heading higher in a hurry.

OIL SHOCK SURPRISE?

Today, many of our traditional supply basins are starting to decline, with less and less oil coming from these critical lifelines each and every year. In America, the birthplace of the oil era, production peaked at 9.6 million barrels per day in 1970 and volumes have been declining ever since. The Norwegian and U.K. North Sea fields have been diminishing since 1999, and so too has Mexico's massive Cantarell oil field, which saw its peak production of 3 million barrels per day back in 2003. In 2008, Indonesia was kicked out of OPEC for becoming—of all things—an oil *importer*.[10]

Russia was looking good for a while, but its production is starting to falter. How about our buddies the Saudis? They have plenty of oil, right? Perhaps, but they still won't let outside experts conduct an audit of their fields, so we can't be certain. In fact, the amount of oil the Saudis claim to have hasn't budged in the last forty years. Lucky? Maybe, but that may be too much to hope for.

Complicating things further is the fact that we don't just have to drill to find more oil to satisfy demand that continues to grow, we also have to keep drilling to *replace* the oil production that is lost through the natural depletion or declining production of the oil fields as they age. According to the International Energy Agency (IEA)*, the depletion rate of oil fields around the world in 2007 stood at 6.7 per cent and is anticipated to increase to 8.6 per cent between now and 2030. Decline rates everywhere are accelerating rapidly as existing oil fields run dry and newer fields are consistently smaller and less prolific. To meet the current decline rate, the world must discover at least another Saudi Arabia every other year just to keep production growth flat.[11]

---

*The International Energy Agency (IEA) is an intergovernmental organization that acts as an energy policy advisor to twenty-eight member countries in their effort to ensure reliable, affordable and clean energy for their citizens. Founded during the oil crisis of 1973–74, the IEA's role was to coordinate measures in times of oil supply emergencies. Source: IEA website: http://www.iea.org/about/index.asp.

FINDING LIQUID GOLD

Our search for tomorrow's oil will continue to take us farther and farther afield. New oil discoveries tend to be in remote and often inhospitable environments. Bitumen coming from Alberta's oil sands requires expensive upgrading to convert into a synthetic crude oil that can be shipped out by pipeline or refined further into gasoline. Alaska holds some promise as a future supply basin, but first it needs to be extensively explored. The state may contain as much as 35 trillion cubic feet of natural gas, but there is currently no pipeline capacity to bring this to market. Alaska's oil supply is just seven hundred thousand barrels a day, a pittance in comparison to the more than 85 million daily barrels the world demands. Offshore Brazil is another area that holds promise of significant future production, but the oil fields that have been discovered there so far lie several hundred kilometres offshore. What's more, UBS estimates that developing just two of Brazil's offshore fields—the Tupi and Carioca—will cost more than $600 billion.[12]

Lack of viable alternatives is the reason why otherwise sane people are pouring billions of dollars into Alberta in the laborious attempt to separate oil from sand. So costly is the process that new oil sands projects now need to have prices between $80 and $90 per barrel or higher to justify the investment. Salaries, steel, just about everything you can imagine costs more, not to mention housing, which now averages just under $700,000 in Fort McMurray. The recent sharp downturn in prices was cause for the cancellation of planned capacity increases in the oil sands of more than 1 million barrels a day. But as slumping prices start making unconventional projects uneconomic, we are setting up the world for another massive oil shock, one that will see prices move up beyond their previous highs and settle in the high $90 per barrel to low $100 per barrel.

To meet the challenge of slumping conventional supply and growing demand, unconventional oil reservoirs like Alberta's, or Venezuela's Orinoco, extra-heavy-oil belt will be ramped up. It will be these basins, where the marginal cost of supply is in the $90 per barrel range and higher, that will set the new floor price for oil. Only when marginal supply and marginal demand come into balance will a long-term price be established. In the meantime, oil prices must move beyond the floor price of the marginal producer ($90 per barrel) to encourage that production to be brought on.

Unfortunately, the IEA has warned that existing oil reservoirs are set to experience a dramatic drop-off in production as they continue to age. It also forecasts that the difference between supply and anticipated demand will need to be met by yet-to-be discovered oil fields, natural gas liquids and unconventional oil, such as synthetic crude oil from Alberta's oil sands.

Natural Gas Liquids (NGLs) are another part of the energy supply chain that the IEA has pointed to as a potential stopgap for meeting rising demand. While propane, butane and pentane are useful hydro-carbons, they won't get your car rolling. What still matters to the world is light sweet crude oil and precious little of that exists.

As oil supply continues to struggle and demand begins to grow again, oil prices will move higher. Speculators may have driven up oil prices faster and higher than they should otherwise have been, but market forces will soon return them to elevated levels, where they will eventually stay put.

ASIAN AUTO NATIONS

Cars are a status symbol in emerging markets, just as they are here. In Vietnam, if you're young and single, or even if you're not, a brand new motor scooter is *de rigueur*. As in North America, having your own set of wheels represents freedom, social status and sex appeal—a fact not lost on the young men of Ho Chi Minh City who spend each Saturday and Sunday night circling Dong Khoi and Nguyen Hue boulevards on their motorcycles in the hopes of meeting eligible young women.

Jaguar and Range Rover are venerable British brands, right? Not anymore. They are now owned by Tata Motors of India. Car ownership is exploding in the developing world, just as new car purchases are dropping like stones in North America. But it isn't rising levels of wealth that are packing the showrooms of Asia with eager buyers—it's that the cars are cheap. Tata is introducing the Nano, known as the "people's car," in 2009. It will retail for just $2,000, a fraction of the cost of Mercedes' similarly styled Smart car. At a price like that, it's only a matter of time until Nanos start popping up in our neighbours' driveways.

FIGURE 10.2 Looking Good for Only $2,000

Source: Getty Images

IN NEED OF A GUSHER

In the years ahead, the developing world will consume more, not less, oil. Canada's climate and sprawling cities make our energy intensity among the highest in the world on a per capita basis—each one of us consuming, on average, 25 barrels of oil per year. In contrast, the Chinese consume just 2.5 barrels per year, a number sure to rise as more people hit the roads in Beijing, Xian and Shanghai.

But what's really driving oil consumption in the developing world is industrialization. Sure, a boatload of new drivers is a big deal, but an even bigger deal is the number of factories and power plants needed to industrialize and urbanize the place. And while those factories and power plants may be belching out smoke, they are also creating a ton of jobs for the millions of farmers who have migrated to the cities in search of a better life.

The IEA predicts that the projected global demand for energy between now and 2030—pegged at 104 barrels per day—will be "unsustainable." Declines are predicted for North America and Europe, but offsetting that will be huge surges in demand from Asia and the Middle East. According to a recent IEA report, China will account for 43 per cent of the new demand, the Middle East and India 20 per cent, and the other emerging Asian economies contributing most of the rest.[13] The growth in oil supply necessary to meet demand will need to come from Middle East OPEC countries, since they are the only ones that have any appreciable spare capacity. Taking into account the predicted declines in existing oil fields, to satisfy future demand the world must find the equivalent of six times the 2008 production of Saudi Arabia between now and 2030—a stunning and sobering task.[14]

I'LL PICK UP THE CHEQUE

What you don't pay for, you don't value; it's an old saying proven true in many oil-producing countries, where subsidization has created a new breed of consumer that just doesn't care about the costs of energy. In societies where consumers pay market price for goods and services, price increases cause obvious, immediate changes in consumer behaviour. In many of the producing countries where consumers are protected by subsidies, however, that pricing signal just isn't being sent.

North Americans are quick to complain when gas prices hit $1.40 per litre, but if you never pay anywhere near the prevailing market rate why would you care what the world price is? You wouldn't. There are countries where rock-bottom energy prices are considered a God-given right. Iran is one of those places. So are Saudi Arabia, Mexico and Venezuela, all of them major oil-producing nations where gas prices get as low as three cents a litre. These are countries whose national treasuries are awash with dollars as a result of high oil prices, which, in turn, have allowed their governments to massively subsidize gas prices at the pump. And rock-bottom prices have resulted in just what you might expect: a massive surge in demand for cheap fuel. With demand skyrocketing, governments that have chosen to subsidize the cost of a fill-up have been saddled with obligations totalling in the billions of dollars a year.

For some of these countries, the cost of subsidizing their citizens has gotten out of hand. In May 2007, Iran made the decision to bump the price of a litre of gas from 800 rials per litre (US$0.30 per gallon) to 1,000 rials. The result was mayhem and riots in downtown Tehran. Needless to say, government officials thought better of it and decided to shelve the plan.

The same is true throughout the Middle East, where subsidies have led to an insatiable demand for gasoline among consumers. In most of the countries that offer these generous subsidies, the leadership cares less about investing back into the industry to develop it further than about the enormous wealth that the industry generates. Placating citizens with cheap oil is all part of the game.

Yet Iran, in spite of being a large energy producer, imports more than 50 per cent of its gasoline. Why? Because it's a bad trade to refine oil into gasoline and then sell that gasoline into a market where you only get cents on the dollar for your product. The Iranians have realized that a better idea is to sell oil on the world market, take those massive profits, and buy all the gasoline they need.

That works, provided you can make a whole lot more selling oil on the world market than the cost of your gasoline subsidy program. But all that is going to change when the predicted demographic explosion that will occur over the next twenty years in the producing regions forces them to prioritize supplying oil to their citizens over oil exports. All of a sudden the subsidies will run smack into increasing waves of domestic consumers who will stretch the local treasuries to the breaking point. Oil demand will skyrocket in many of the producing countries, as subsidies and robust population growth underpin a rapid rise in demand in the Middle East, Venezuela and Mexico. With leadership unwilling to chance massive civil unrest, the bottom line is that subsidies are here to stay in the producing countries.

HEADING WEST

The Alberta oil sands region is the largest industrial complex in the world, covering an area approximately the size of Florida. Millions of years ago, the area was a boreal forest and wetlands, but time and pressure converted it into the massive oil reserve it is today. And while there are better oil and gas basins in the world, none can match the long reserve life and political stability of Alberta. While much has been made of the demise of Ontario's auto sector, Canadian energy exports topped automotive exports as the single biggest export category from 2006 to 2008. Huge amounts of investment poured into the province—home to two-thirds of the country's oil and gas—when oil prices were edging higher, and Alberta is destined to become the economic heart of Canada again when the crisis passes and oil prices steady.

The oil sands are not just ground zero for the oil industry in Canada, however; they're the whole shooting match. In terms of our national oil reserves, it is the oil sands plus a rounding error—the conventional reserves amounting to very little. With more than 173 billion barrels of crude, Alberta boasts the second-largest oil reserves globally after Saudi Arabia.

But beyond the product, what Canada also has going for it is ready access to the largest oil consumer in the world: the United States. It's important to realize that when U.S. politicians talk about kicking their addiction to foreign oil, they aren't talking about getting less Canadian crude—they are talking about ridding themselves of their dependence on the Middle East. America imports approximately 60 per cent of the oil it consumes, with Canada supplying more of it than any other country. In 2004, we overtook Saudi Arabia as the leading crude supplier to the United States—a status we won't be relinquishing any time soon. Canada is already the third-largest exporter of natural gas[15] and the seventh-largest oil producer in the world and, if future development initiatives get back on track, we could break into the top four.

When energy prices were surging, Alberta's per capita gross domestic product became the highest in the country, clocking in at 160 per cent of the national average. What's more, Alberta's gains appear to be Ontario's and Quebec's losses, the two provinces having given up more than 350,000 manufacturing jobs combined since 2002.[16] As production from the oil sands moves to 3 million barrels per day from 1 million between now and 2020, the industry is expected to create more than 5 million person years of employment. And most of those jobs—some four out of five—are expected to be created *outside* of the energy sector.[17]

Pipelines are another segment of the economy with promise for job creation and investment opportunities. With future increases in oil sands production, and upgrading costs in Alberta three times what they are south of the border, the push is on to bring Alberta bitumen or crude south to Texas, the refining heartland of America. Some of the players scrambling to get a piece of the action include Enbridge Inc., which is working on a pipeline proposal with Exxon Mobil Corp. In the energy boom of 2007 and 2008, workers were flocking to Alberta in search of high-paying jobs. In the boom's heyday, managers of fast-food restaurants could pull in up to $60,000 per year, while Wal-Mart offered bonuses to employees who stayed with the company for more than a thousand days.[18] The coming boom in oil prices will lift the fortunes of a far wider swath of Albertans—everyone from burger flippers to barmaids to hotel workers—not simply those employees directly engaged in the energy sector.

I have visited the oil sands several times, and each time I'm awed by its immense scope. The mining operations of Syncrude and Suncor, with their fleet of massive dump trucks ferrying back and forth, are truly staggering. The largest trucks weigh more than a 747 airplane and cost over $5 million. Standing next to one is a humbling experience, given that the tires alone are four metres in diameter. More than 80 per cent of the oil reserves lie too far beneath the earth's surface (at depths of fifty metres or more) to be mined and must be extracted using a process known as Steam Assisted Gravity Drainage (SAGD). When I visited Petro-Canada's* MacKay River project in 2007, I was floored by the amount of steel piping and well pairs ringing the property. Getting this precious resource out of the ground is no small undertaking.

Over the next decade, more than $100 billion will be spent to further develop the oil sands. The *National Post* has cited independent studies estimating that, between 2000 and 2020, oil sands development will generate at least $123 billion in royalty and tax revenues for Canadian governments and boost total Canadian GDP by $789 billion.[19] It's the kind of heft that will transform Canada into an energy superpower and provide strong job growth for decades to come.

PUMP UP YOUR PORTFOLIO

Unless you think the world is going to end, or that the average Chinese or Indian individual isn't going to own a car—ever—then you would be crazy not to be buying into great national energy stocks such as Canadian Natural Resources Ltd. or Canadian Oil Sands Trust (the operator of the Syncrude project). For direct exposure to oil sands and the best management team in the industry, look no further than Suncor Energy. The company first started operating along a swath of the Athabasca River in 1967, and today boasts a long reserve life and a solid balance sheet and has just merged with Petro-Canada—making

---

*On March 23, 2009, Suncor and Petro-Canada announced their intention to merge and form a new energy company.

it a global energy major. So while the rest of your peers fret about the slowing global economy, you can slowly, and confidently, place your bets on the continuing global growth story by buying a slice of oil sands production. Not only are they levered to the best supply basin in the world, but they aren't under the control of a hostile government like 90 per cent of the globe oil reserves.

Another approach is to buy shares in larger-capitalization exploration and production (E&P) companies, whose share prices have the greatest leverage to rising oil prices. Not only this, but they are a lot less risky than the junior energy companies, which are too thinly traded and often have very marginal projects to develop. While rising oil prices will lift all boats, the first to respond will be the senior E&P names, such as Canadian Natural Resources, followed next by the oil sands producers.

The integrated oil companies, the ones with refineries and gas stations, such as Petro-Canada and Imperial Oil Ltd., will do well also, but their performance will tend to get dragged down by the lower-margin refining business. Petro-Canada's share price is also limited by the Petro-Canada Public Participation Act, which prohibits the sale of the company to non-Canadian residents, limits ownership stakes to 20 per cent and mandates that the head office remain in Calgary. So while Petro-Canada generally trades at a discount to its peers, there's a reason for it. The company also has a history of overspending on large energy projects which, combined with the Petro-Canada Public Participation Act, makes a shakeup at the top unrealistic.[20]

One of the best ways to get leverage to rising oil prices is through companies in the energy services sector, such as Precision Drilling Trust, Ensign Energy Services Inc. and Calfrac Well Services Ltd. As the global energy industry evolved, energy companies such as EnCana and Talisman Energy Inc. found that it didn't make great economic sense to maintain a fleet of drilling rigs and well-fracturing specialists. The result was that divisions were spun out of larger companies to create the energy services industry—basically, contractors for hire. It's a business much more volatile than oil and gas itself, since contractors are always the first to be cut when a slowdown occurs in the industry. Oil and gas producers start spending more money when they're confident that higher prices are here to stay, and when this happens, the prices for energy service companies can really rise.

Food, plastics, chemicals, cosmetics, rubber and other oil-based products get a whole lot more expensive to produce when oil prices are high. The chemical industry is a case in point. Since oil is a critical raw material in chemical production, higher oil prices translate into lower margins and tough times for chemical companies. Investors should thus avoid the shares of chemical companies when the oil bull returns.

MIRACLE FUEL

While we may wish it weren't the case, we are still very much living in the petroleum era. The day is coming when once again demand will be strong and supply tight, and when that happens oil prices will be headed higher, and for longer, than anyone may have yet thought possible. Drivers may grumble, but investors in the energy sector will be richly rewarded for the higher prices at the pump.

There is no substitute for oil; it makes our modern world possible. Oil shocks have come and gone and public interest in energy prices has ebbed and flowed, but this time we are entering the perfect storm for sustained higher oil prices. In the aftermath of this crisis, oil prices will surge and remain elevated for a very long time, and energy investors will make out like bandits.

CHAPTER SUMMARY

- When oil prices are high, the broad economy is struggling and most of the stock market is for sale.
- Oil prices will be higher in the future because demand continues to grow, particularly from parts of the world where gasoline prices are subsidized.

- Supply and demand is the only thing that matters to the long-run pricing of oil.
- E&P companies offer the best leverage to rising oil prices, and in the later stages of the rally, junior oil and gas companies and services companies should be bought.
- Our world will look dramatically different in the era of high oil prices.

11

DIGGING FOR DOUGH: INVESTING IN METALS AND MINES

Canada is a mining superstar, but you'd hardly know it after the beating our companies have taken. No sector is as levered to the twists and turns of the global economy as the price of metals and the shares of global mining companies. As world economic activity started to evaporate, traders everywhere began pushing the sell button on metals and the companies that produce them. Fortunes changed overnight: seasoned executives ran for cover, miners lost their shirts and Russian oligarchs hung for-sale signs on their assets, dragging the ruble to its lowest level in years in the process. Booms and busts are to be expected in this sector, but this time around it was blindsided by a sucker punch; no one saw that a meltdown in one segment of the U.S. housing market would so quickly lead to the complete collapse of the global economy. Shovels were dropped on the spot as mining executives stared in disbelief at their plummeting stock prices. Production quickly ground to a halt and mines were closed in short order.

But rising like the proverbial phoenix from the ashes of all this financial ruin, a clear winner has nevertheless emerged: Canada, which, with its global mining companies, devastated competition and solid banks, will soon be in the ideal position to capitalize on a resurgent metals industry.

THE BIG DIG

Mining is cyclical, with long bull markets followed by years of slumping sales. For most of the 1980s and 1990s, mining just wasn't growing as a business. Then, in 2002, after years of being in the doldrums, it started to come alive, driven by strong economic growth everywhere and the rapid urbanization of China and India. Prices for metals doubled, then tripled. There seemed to be no limit to the heights they could attain. Large mining companies got larger: Brazilian mining giant Vale snapped up Canada's Inco, and Xstrata bought Falconbridge.

Hedge funds, mutual funds and day traders joined the fray in the belief that this would be a super cycle for the base metals. After all, the Chinese demand seemed insatiable and growth everywhere else looked pretty solid as well. The prices for stocks and commodities headed higher, prompting companies such as Xstrada to base its operating strategies on the mantra "stronger for longer."* In February of 2008, BHP Billiton, an Anglo-Australian mining company that already is the largest of its kind in the world, almost created a veritable behemoth by bidding for Rio Tinto, the third-largest player in the industry. While the deal was never consummated, the motivation was obvious: achieve massive economies of scale and enormous bargaining power with customers, and reduce reliance on a single commodity.

In mining, size and scale *really* matter. Everything about mining is enormous, from the holes punched in the ground to the equipment

---

*Xstrata's "stronger for longer" mantra refers to the strength of the commodity cycle.

used to extract minerals from the earth's surface. In contract negotiations during January 2008, Vale was able to use its considerable heft to push through a 65 per cent increase in iron ore prices to desperate steelmakers for the upcoming contract year.[1]

Mining is also big business. In 2007, it accounted for nearly four hundred thousand jobs in Canada and added $42 billion to our gross domestic product.[2] For a while, the mining companies had it good. And so did many Sudbury, Ontario miners who, back in 2007 when metals prices were on fire, could make upwards of $150,000 a year when their salaries and nickel bonuses were tallied—the nickel bonus being a form of profit-sharing paid out to miners when the price of nickel moved beyond a certain price and the company achieved profit targets.[3]

During the industry's heyday, it wasn't just Sudbury's miners who did well; some of the area's twelve thousand service sector workers also experienced unprecedented success. When the price of nickel hit an all-time high of $23.40 per pound, they bought up fishing boats, Jet Skis, snowmobiles and trucks like they were going out of style. But when nickel prices eventually came off hard, hitting $5.30 per pound by the end of 2008, the good times at mining camps like Sudbury's quickly became a thing of the past. Globally, more than $1 trillion in equity value has been eviscerated from mining shares since March 2008.

MATERIAL WORLD

Metals and mining have shaped our world for thousands of years. As countries move from agrarian societies to industrialized societies, people move from farms to cities and create, along the way, huge demand for things like homes, cars and appliances. This in turn drives the need for factories that turn out all the things people need to make the move from the fields to the factory floor. Nowhere has this process been more visible than in China, which is experiencing a rate of urbanization of 1 per cent annually. That's 13 million new urbanites the Chinese have to provide housing and appliances to each year.

In America, there is a 50 per cent chance when you flip on the light switch that the electricity in your home is generated in a coal-fired generating plant. If you happen to live in France, however, where more than 78 per cent of the electricity is generated in nuclear plants, then uranium is what has produced your power.

Depending on the application, there's a metal or a combination of metals that's right for the job. Iron ore, the most commonly used metal, is what steel is made from. About 66 per cent of all steel is produced in mills using blast furnace technology that consumes coking coal, also known as metallurgical coal. With its superior strength, steel has long played a supporting role in the building, construction and automotive industries. Modern skyscrapers are made with steel girders that form the frame, while the subway cars you ride to work in have a steel chassis. Steel prices are strongly tied to rising global industrial production. When the world's industries are humming away at a strong clip, then steel prices are sure to be on the rise.

Copper has been around for millennia and was used to produce weapons and tools during the Bronze Age. Today it's used primarily in the building and construction industries. According to consultancy Bloomsbury Minerals Economics Limited, almost 50 per cent of copper is consumed in the world's factories.[4] The firm predicts that for 2009 and beyond, the emerging markets will account for most of the new copper consumption. Copper also has extensive use in electronic applications, and thus its price is overwhelmingly driven by consumer behaviour; copper prices get moving when that boatload of flat screen televisions and home computers at your local Best Buy start moving out of the store.

You may not realize it when you hoist a beer can to your lips, but the aluminum that the can is made from is the second most common metal around. At only one-third the weight of steel and with better corrosion resistance, aluminum is used to make aircraft parts and door frames and in high-performance applications such as high-end car bodies or sports equipment.

Nickel is used to produce stainless steel, a metal known for its strength and corrosion resistance and used in everything from aerospace applications to the kitchen sink. Zinc can be combined with steel to produce galvanized steel, a corrosion-fighting, stronger form of steel often used as reinforcing bars (construction) and for roofs. It's also used in the automotive industry as the outer skin of most cars and trucks. Lead is used primarily in car and motorcycle batteries and, of course, bullets.

Metals matter to our everyday lives, but because the process of urbanizing and industrializing is extremely metals-intensive they are even more critical to the developing world, which consumes four to five times the quantity of metals per unit output as does the West.

CHINA IS DRIVING THE DEMAND BUS

China is the eight-hundred-pound gorilla of metals demand, accounting for roughly one-third of the total for aluminum, copper, nickel and zinc. China and India combined demand more than two and a half times the amount of metals as America and, with China continuing to act as the world's factory, this will only increase in the future. In January 2009, with U.S. car production slipping for the first time in history, China sold more cars than America.[5] Without a single export, China is already the world's second-biggest car manufacturer, and it's only a matter of time before it takes the top spot.[6] In 2007, China consumed 28 per cent of the world's steel and 57 per cent of its coking coal. And its emerging dominance in car manufacturing and growing middle class will make it a big demand driver behind steel and iron ore prices over the next ten years.

As with all the metals China consumes, growth in consumption has been truly staggering. In 1990, China represented 7.5 per cent of global zinc consumption, but by 2007, the number was up to 32 per cent, half of which ended up as the galvanized steel rods and roofs used around the world by contractors in buildings large and small. The story is the same for copper; during the height of the commodity bull market in 2007, China accounted for almost 100 per cent of its global demand growth, according to Barclay's Capital.

Lead producers will be the ones to benefit from China's e-bike, a popular replacement for the motorcycle—and almost as powerful—that runs entirely on battery power. With more than 80 million e-bikes on the road and sales of more than 20 million a year rolling off the assembly lines, this phenomenon is here to stay. And at $250, the e-bike is priced right. It's the perfect solution for high gas prices and great news for buyers of lead or lead-producing companies, since 81 per cent of lead is used in batteries.

FIGURE 11.1 Stylish and for Only $250

Source: Getty Images

MITTAL, THE METALS MAN

India is no bit player when it comes to global demand for steel, iron ore and coking coal. According to CRU, a U.K.-based consultancy, India and Brazil are expected to be the only countries *increasing* imports of coking coal in 2009. The firm predicts that the bulk of coking coal imports from now to 2019 will be driven by Asia—particularly India. Of a total seaborne market that CRU estimates will grow to more than 320 million tonnes in 2019, India will account for more than 52 million tonnes.

India's influence as a steel producer is growing, in part, because of the remarkable success of steel company Arcelor Mittal. Headed by Indian-born tycoon Lakshmi Mittal, Arcelor Mittal became the world's largest steel company in 2006. In building his massive empire, Mittal chose to break from the traditional nationalist steel company model and build a truly global company. It used to be that every country felt it had to have its own national steel giant, regardless of whether it made any money or not. Arcelor Mittal tried something different: it brought modern management thinking and a global perspective to the table. Of the top thirty executives in the firm, nine different nationalities are represented. And the company does more than use its size to acquire smaller rivals, it continually monitors its business practices by benchmarking how it is doing against leaders in other fields, such as Royal Dutch Shell on information technology practices.[7] In the process, Mittal—with 10 per cent of world steel output—has become the industry's only truly global producer.

THE NEW NUKES

Nuclear power used to be an industry in decline as worries over safety—typified by the 1979 film *The China Syndrome*—spooked Americans into demanding the closure of many of America's nuclear plants. One such project that I learned about when I worked at Enron was the Shoreham Nuclear Power Plant, near Brookhaven, New York, in Long Island Sound. The plant was developed by the Long Island Lighting Company (LILCO), one of my customers at the time. The construction of Shoreham was announced in 1965, with construction costs estimated to be between $65 million and $75 million and a schedule aimed at getting the facility online in 1973. However, poor worker productivity and constant design changes demanded by the Nuclear Regulatory Commission (NRC) caused the cost of the project to balloon to more than $2 billion.

Then, in March 1979, a partial core meltdown occurred at the Unit 2 reactor in the Three Mile Island Nuclear Generating Station near Harrisburg, Pennsylvania. In June, the largest demonstration in Long Island history saw fifteen thousand protestors gathered by the main gates of the Shoreham plant. Police arrested more than six hundred people trying to scale the fence in an attempt to gain access.

The result was universal opposition to the construction by local politicians, including New York governor Mario Cuomo, who led the charge to close the plant. Despite the opposition, the plant was completed in 1984, but politicians and local community groups refused to sign a necessary evacuation plan for the facility, which effectively denied LILCO an operating licence. Finally, on February 28, 1989, Governor Cuomo and LILCO announced plans to decommission the plant. Shoreham had run for just four hours and cost more than $6 billion to construct.

Today, however, with concerns mounting over climate change, nuclear power is enjoying a renaissance. Presently there are 439 nuclear power plants in operation, supplying about 17 per cent of the world's power requirements. France is at the forefront of the nuclear power industry, generating approximately 78 per cent of its power this way. With nuclear power back on the agenda, uranium soared to a high of $138 per pound in June 2007 from approximately $14 per pound in 2004.[8] One of the beneficiaries of the buzz was Saskatoon-based Cameco, the largest producer of uranium in the world, supplying 16 per cent of the global demand. Recently, the company has had some operational challenges, such as the flooding at its McArthur River mine. It also continues to struggle with its Cigar Lake project, the world's largest undeveloped high-grade uranium deposit. But in spite of these difficulties, the company still has world-class assets and remains one of the most important producers of uranium.

The Cigar Lake mine is expected to reach full production in 2016 and when that happens it will represent approximately 8 per cent of global consumption.

PASS THE VODKA

As the financial crisis evolved, metals dropped from their peak prices by anywhere between 60 and 82 per cent, taking the fortunes of traders, mining executives and oligarchs down the drain. Traders followed the playbook perfectly, selling the metals down as fast as they could when things in the global economy started to look dicey. Perhaps no one was more surprised by the speed with which the meltdown in the U.S. subprime housing market hit the metals market, however, than the Russian oligarchs: a group of around thirty gangster capitalists who bought or brutalized their way to fabulous wealth by snagging the crown jewels of industrial Russia during the breakup of the Soviet Union.

The oligarchs first came to prominence under Boris Yeltsin, who became the first popularly elected president of the Russian Soviet Federative Socialist Republic in June 1991. With the dissolution of the Soviet Union in December of that year, Yeltsin vowed to transform Russia into a modern free-market economy. He liberalized prices on goods and services and privatized many of the country's major industries in a series of rigged auctions. For a select few, who bribed or bludgeoned the right people to gain control of the most lucrative sectors of the economy, Yeltsin was a dream come true. In exchange for political and economic support, he allowed the oligarchs to grow fabulously wealthy.

At the height of the market in 2007, the oligarchs' extravagance knew no limits. Dmitry Rybolovlev, the Russian fertilizer king, scooped up Donald Trump's Palm Beach mansion for about $100 million. Roman Abramovich, a steel and oil magnate, is well known for his ownership of a small armada of yachts—many 150 metres or more in length—and for buying the Chelsea Football Club. Oleg Deripaska, once considered the richest man in Russia, amassed a fortune of nearly $28 billion before the crash. His company, Basic Element, became Russia's largest industrial conglomerate and, in 2008, he invested $1.5 billion in Magna International, the Canadian auto parts maker. With a business empire based on large-scale borrowing, Deripaska was ripe for a fall. By the summer of 2008, he had to forfeit his investment in Magna when he was unable to meet a margin call as the stock fell. United Company RUSAL, the crown jewel of his empire and the largest aluminum producer in the world, was saved from certain bankruptcy by a last-minute $4.5 billion loan from Vnesheconombank, a state-controlled bank. So severe have been Deripaska's losses that some people are even speculating that he is no longer a billionaire.

Norilsk Nickel, the largest nickel producer in the world, was almost bankrupt in the mid-1990s. In 1997, the firm was privatized when Mikhail Prokhorov and Vladimir Potanin took the helm, transforming the once moribund firm into an efficient producer of nickel and palladium, a rare metal most often used in catalytic converters, by slashing costs and trimming overhead. At the top of the market, Prokhorov showed some savvy market timing by dumping his 25 per cent stake in Norilsk and selling it to Oleg Deripaska's United Company RUSAL. As Norilsk Nickel's largest shareholder, Potanin has seen his holdings in the company slide more than 80 per cent and he is now trying to obtain Moscow's help for a bailout of the company.

Moscow will no doubt use the current downturn in the metals markets to regain control over some of the country's crown jewels. The Russian people resent the oligarchs' excessive wealth and many suspect that they looted their way to the top. Vladimir Putin put them on notice during his 2000 election campaign by saying that as a class the oligarchs would cease to exist. In May 2005, Mikhail Khodorkovsky—the wealthiest man in Russia at the time, having built his fortune running oil giant Yukos—was convicted of fraud and income tax evasion and sentenced to eight years in a Siberian prison. But Khodorkovsky's real crime may have been his active interest in supporting political parties other than Vladimir Putin's. As the downturn in the global economy continues, it is a certainty that Putin and Co. will increase their control over the assets of the once mighty oligarchs.[9]

SHIP TO SHORE

You don't have to be a vodka-and-caviar-swilling oligarch to have suffered from the meltdown of metals prices. Lots of ordinary investors took it on the chin and so too did the major mining companies forced to shut down some of their less economical projects. BHP Billiton stopped pursuing the acquisition of Rio Tinto, and Xstrata PLC abandoned plans to acquire Lonmin PLC, the world's third-largest platinum producer. With banks in no mood to lend, companies such as Canada's Vancouver-based Teck Cominco, which loaded up on a boatload of debt when it snapped up Fording Canadian Coal Trust for a cool $14 billion, have seen share prices suffer as investors fret over their survival.[10] For small junior mining companies operating just a single mine, the situation has been a whole lot worse, with their herd now dramatically thinned.

Metal prices and mining companies are due for a recovery, but when? You don't have to be Aristotle Onassis to prosper from knowledge of what is happening on the high seas. Almost 90 per cent of all cargo, metals being no exception, is transported by ship, making the Baltic Dry Index—which measures changes in the cost to ship raw materials including metals, grain and oil—one smart way for us land-lubbers to monitor the health of the global economy. Steel will be the first metal to move higher in price and, when that happens, you can be sure that the Baltic Dry Index will be moving hand in glove along with it.

FIGURE 11.2 The Baltic Dry Index: Not All Wet

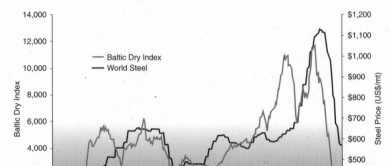

Once steel prices start heading higher, coking coal prices will follow in lockstep. This will be great news for Teck Cominco, Canada's largest diversified mining company, which operates six coal mines in western Canada and is the second-largest exporter of seaborne hard-coking coal in the world.[11] As global trade begins to pick up and global economic activity begins to surge, zinc prices will turn up next, and with them the fortunes of Toronto's HudBay Minerals Inc., a major, cash-rich zinc miner with a resource base that should extend until 2020 and beyond.[12] Copper prices, on the other hand, will likely lag the other metals until late 2010. First Quantum Minerals Ltd. of Vancouver, a growing mining and metals company with a focus on copper production in Mauritania, Finland and the Democratic Republic of Congo, could be one of the beneficiaries of a copper upturn.[13]

Investors looking to get broad exposure to the eventual upswing in metals prices can also consider the Horizons BetaPro S&P/TSX Global Mining Bull Plus ETF, which provides exposure to an underlying basket of global mining equities. This particular product tries to replicate the performance of the S&P/TSX Global Mining Index, offering double its daily performance.[14] This is a very good way to increase your exposure to the sector while avoiding single-name concentration issues. Of course, the double exposure can also be a double-edged sword: it's great when things are moving your way, but it may leave you feeling like a Russian oligarch if things turn south.

CHAPTER SUMMARY

- The financial mayhem hit metal prices hard, sending mining shares plummeting downward.
- Steel, iron ore and coking coal prices are driven by global industrial production.
- Lead demand is driven by battery sales and should get a boost from China's popular e-bike.
- Construction activity drives up zinc prices; copper prices are strongly linked to consumer behaviour.
- A sustained rise in the Baltic Dry Index is a signal to increase your exposure to steel, iron ore, coking coal and zinc.
- Copper prices will lag the recovery of the other metals.

12

FOOD FIGHT: FOOD INFLATION AND HOW TO PROFIT FROM IT

Farming the world over has remained largely untouched by the rapid globalization that has transformed industries such as high tech and even steel. Government protectionism and subsidies have sheltered farmers from the realities of the marketplace, and have served to entrench inefficient agricultural practices. We have already seen significant worldwide increases in the price of food, but inefficient production, rapid urbanization, low levels of grain stocks and increasing levels of wealth will be sending food prices even higher in the years to come. But there's a bright side. A surging global middle class, changing diets and natural limits on the amount of arable land all add up to make a compelling case for agricultural investing. Unlike other commodities whose demand depends on the health of the global economy, the agricultural sector is immune to the vagaries of the business cycle. And Saskatchewan, with the best deposits of potash anywhere in the world, will be a huge beneficiary as the global demand for food grows.

TRADING PLACES

Farming is an uncertain business. Weather and crop prices are volatile, which can severely affect a farmer's finances. As far back as 1848, farmers and businessmen in the Chicago area recognized the problem and eighty-two merchants banded together to create the Chicago Board of Trade (CBOT). Chicago was a logical place to try to manage the trade in grain. It offered rail links and shipping access through the Great Lakes, but most importantly, it was near the heart of farming—the U.S. Midwest. By matching up buyers and sellers of agricultural products, the farmer finally had a solution to the dilemma of price uncertainty: selling his future crop *forward* for a set price to a food processor or other middleman who was also looking for price certainty.[1]

Agricultural commodities also seemed like a good deal to the pension and hedge funds that saw these relatively small markets as ripe for the picking during the great agricultural bull market of 2000 to 2008. While agriculture and energy markets in the U.S. are regulated by the Commodity Futures Trading Commission (CFTC), they have taken a laissez-faire approach to regulation since 1992. The agricultural market has long been recognized as a relatively small market where speculative activity should be strictly limited to prevent violent price swings from distorting the markets—a situation that could potentially price farmers and food processors out of the market entirely. Concern over the level of speculative activity in agricultural commodities drove the thinking at the CFTC for more than seventy-five years, with strict limitations imposed on the quantity of agriculture futures that speculators could amass.

Under Wendy Gramm's leadership, beginning in 1988, however, the CFTC began to show greater flexibility in interpreting the strict letter of the law in commodities. The new logic dictated that if an investment bank happened to be buying agricultural futures on behalf of a pension fund that was looking for exposure to agricultural prices, then *perhaps* it wasn't necessarily speculation. The rationale that the CFTC used was an extension of the principle that they used to regulate agricultural commodities in the first place: namely, that outright speculation was bad, but hedging was fine. Because investment banks participated with pension funds and others in complicated transactions called "swaps," the investment banks were able to effectively argue that the futures positions they were taking were in fact *hedges* for other positions they had on their books and therefore not outright speculation on the direction of futures. While the CFTC had given banks and brokerage firms favourable assurances that this was how they would view these transactions, it wasn't until 1992 that the U.S. government passed legislation giving the CFTC the jurisdictional authority to rule on the appropriateness of such transactions. Armed with its new legal authority, the CFTC wasted no time in handing out exemptions to various companies, including Enron Corp. In 1993, with the inauguration of President Bill Clinton, Wendy Gramm submitted her resignation and left the CFTC. Five weeks later she joined the board of directors of Enron Corp.

The door that the CFTC propped open helped pension funds and hedge funds gain largely unfettered access to commodity markets that used to restrict speculative activity. One detractor of the CFTC's regulation-light approach was Philip McBride Johnson, a former chairman of the agency. In testifying before a congressional committee, McBride Johnson commented that "with the CFTC's withdrawal from regulating many of the more popular derivatives in the late 1980's and early 1990's, it appeared that dealers in those financial products had found a virtually regulation-free promised land."[2]

His assertions would seem to ring true. In 2000, the total exposure of long-only speculative buyers in commodity futures was just $4.7 billion, according to Gersham Investments, a New York-based fund specializing in commodities. But, by the beginning of 2008, the speculative buying activity on American exchanges had zoomed to $260 billion.

One of the first pension funds to discover the new religion of commodity investing was the Ontario Teachers' Pension Plan. From an initial toe-dipping of $100 million in 1997, it quickly increased its exposure, becoming one of the world's largest investors in commodities with approximately $3 billion in commodity investments.[3]

While energy likely grabbed the lion's share of the commodity investing dollars during this period, there is no doubt that agriculture prices were boosted by strong capital flows into commodity funds. Both farmers and grain elevator operators have seen their finances crimped by the wild price swings of agricultural commodities. While North American farmers may be feeling whipsawed from the price spikes and crashes in the futures markets for soybeans, corn and wheat, they have also been big beneficiaries of rising agricultural prices.

Speculators, encouraged by loose regulation, stampeded into commodities as an indirect way to profit from the growth in the developing world. With the devastation that the wizards of Wall Street wreaked on their own houses—not to mention those of their best clients—the hedge and pension funds' rampant, unfettered speculation in the commodity markets is now yesterday's story. In May 2008, the U.S. Senate passed legislation aimed at closing the Enron Loophole and is also investigating the possibility that the crude oil market may have been manipulated.

HUNGRY PLANET

Behind the hype about rising food prices, however, something very real is happening in the world of food. Changing diets, rapid urbanization and a growing global population are all putting unprecedented stresses on the food chain, meaning more food must be produced between now and 2050 than has been produced during the past ten thousand years combined.[4]

The rapid rise in the price of rice, a dietary staple for half the world's population, is a case in point. Since the beginning of 2007, the price of Thai medium-quality rice—a global benchmark—has more than doubled. Concern over the cost of food has resulted in riots in Egypt and Morocco, while in Thailand, rice farmers have been sleeping in their fields in an attempt to ward off thieves. In the Philippines, the government has made rice hoarding a crime punishable by life imprisonment. Higher food prices have, in turn, led governments to tighten their grip on the food market. In Vietnam and Argentina, governments are capping exports of key foodstuffs to quell inflation at home—sometimes in violation of global trade rules.

The rising food prices of the last few years stand in stark contrast to the previous four decades when food prices were declining. Over the last fifty years, global food production tripled, while the world population doubled and average life expectancy surged from forty-six in the 1950s to a worldwide average of sixty-five today. During this period, output expanded as Western farms became large-scale commercial enterprises, fields were irrigated and artificial fertilizers and pesticides were used to boost yields.

Most countries protect their farmers from competition with a variety of subsidies, quotas and tariffs. When I lived in France, I was struck by the number of times I witnessed farmers block traffic in protests over various European Union agricultural directives. In a country that worships food, French farmers hold enormous sway over the government no matter how wrong-headed their stance is. Farming throughout the world is inefficient and while governments globally push for self-sufficiency in food, the end result is a bizarre situation where farmers are, in many instances, paid *not* to farm. By 2002, food prices started to rise, with real food prices escalating more than 64 per cent by mid-2008.[5]

Higher food prices have translated into more, not fewer, hungry people in this world. According to a 2008 study by the United Nations Food and Agricultural Organization (FAO), the number of hungry globally was estimated at 923 million in 2007—an increase of more than 80 million since 1990–1992. The causes cited include poverty, landless households, the rising cost of food and sluggish government responses to the food crisis. The poor have been hit harder than any other group in society, since the vast majority of them are without land and must therefore rely on purchased food. Higher food prices have the effect of reducing the real income of the poor, forcing them to either compromise on the quantity or quality of their food or resort to more desperate measures to survive.

The bubble that formed around the West in the run-up to the financial crisis was a major contributor to rising food prices. The high correlation between oil and food prices meant that fertilizer nearly tripled in price between 2006 and 2008, while transportation costs doubled. Rising food prices and competition for food and other resources effectively crowded out many of the world's poor. In Ethiopia and Kenya, many farmers were unable to get the necessary credit to finance farm purchases during 2008, so they responded by planting less.

Soaring food prices are more than an inconvenience—they threaten political stability globally. In an integrated world, our neighbours' problems can become our own very quickly. According to the World Bank, some thirty-three countries are now vulnerable to social and political unrest because of food scarcity. In places such as Cameroon and Senegal, as well as other African countries, a large proportion of the population exists on $1 or less a day.[6] Considered the poorest of the poor, those living on this type of subsistence wage number about 2.5 billion worldwide, with an additional 100 million people on the brink of joining their ranks.

Rising food prices will continue to increase the divide between rich and poor in both developed and developing nations. In the poorest regions of the world, food expenditures amount to 70 per cent of the total family budget, which can present a stark choice: riot or starve. And while rioting can bring about a change of government, what happens if power is transferred violently in a poor nation with nuclear weapons? Rising food prices are a big deal for us all.

COULD THE CUPBOARD BE BARE?

An increase in global food prices similar to the one happening today occurred during the Arab oil embargo of the early 1970s. Higher oil prices affect food prices in a couple of important ways: through higher transportation costs in shipping food to market and in rising diesel prices for the tractors and farm equipment that produce the food. Energy represents about 15 per cent of total input costs for the average American farm.[7] More than half of all food sales globally occur in supermarkets, even in the developing world, making transportation and logistics costs a significant expense in getting the food from field to table. At the other end of the food chain, seed and fertilizer companies are affected when oil prices are rising, since higher oil prices influence the cost of producing nitrogen, a fertilizer made from natural gas. As oil and natural gas prices tend to move in tandem, you can be sure that if oil prices are rising, nitrogen—a fertilizer used in 59 per cent of all farm applications—is going to cost more.

A combination of adverse weather and changing agricultural policies in many of the countries that produce cereals (rice, wheat and other coarse grains) has put stockpiles of cereals at a three-decade low. Drought and floods during the 2005 to 2007 growing seasons resulted in world cereal production falling by 3.6 per cent in 2005 and 6.9 per cent in 2006 before staging a modest recovery in 2007. The poor harvests helped to deplete global grain stocks to their current, historically low levels. Now at the lowest level ever recorded, world grain stocks have fallen to just less than eleven weeks of supply (see figure 12.1). Without an adequate inventory of grain, the world is counting on just-in-time grain production to meet its insatiable appetite. Severe drought, frost or other unusual weather event could push food prices higher and send more people globally into poverty.

FIGURE 12.1 Grain Stocks Are at Historic Lows

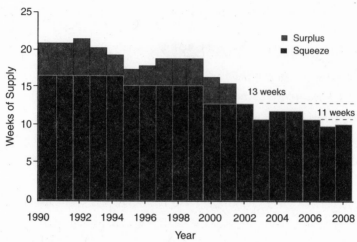

Source: British Sulphur

PLANES, TRAINS AND TRACTORS

In many developing countries, food production is still not a modern commercial undertaking. In China, 92 per cent of farms are subsistence farms and, while most of China's surging food demand has been met domestically, continued growth there and in India will necessitate a change in the way food is produced. Not only is demand for food increasing, but a fundamental shift is occurring in what people in the developing world are eating.

Rising incomes have meant increased consumption of meat and dairy products worldwide, which places greater demands on grains production, since these foods are very grain- and water-intensive to produce. Currently, the most popular meat in the world is chicken. In China, where half the world's pigs are raised and eaten, pork is dominant.[8] It takes between two and seven kilograms of grain to produce just one kilogram of meat. A meat-based diet is so resource-intensive that it takes from two to four times more land for a meat eater's diet than it does for a vegetarian's diet.

Demand for grains will only increase in the years to come as this trend continues and the global population increases. The *Journal of*

Nutrition estimates that by 2020, the global share of meat consumed by the developing world will increase to 63 per cent from 52 per cent.[9] While dietary trends are pointing toward more meat in the global diet, it will take some time before the developing world, which currently consumes twenty-eight kilograms of meat per person annually, matches the whopping eighty kilograms per person that we chew through in the industrialized world. But while the developing world may lag behind us in meat consumption per person, the *overall* rate of meat consumption is nevertheless growing at twice the rate of population growth in the developing world.[10]

Resource scarcity further hampers our ability to meet the increasing needs of a hungry world. Agriculture accounts for 70 per cent of all water usage globally, and just 18 per cent of irrigated cropland is responsible for producing 40 per cent of the world's food. Rice is particularly water-intensive, requiring about three thousand litres to produce just one kilogram of product. Unfortunately, as already mentioned, evaporation and leaky pipes mean that half the water used for irrigation never reaches the crops for which it is intended. Excessive salt buildup is another problem. According to the U.N. FAO, the issue affects 30 million of 240 million acres that are irrigated worldwide.

But farmers' fields are not the only things being affected by the diversion of rivers and lakes for irrigation: fish stocks, the main source of protein for 6 per cent of the world's population, are suffering as well. In Asia alone, fish supplies about 30 per cent of the protein needs of 1 billion people. Areas that have been dammed for irrigation, such as the Mekong Delta in Vietnam, have seen dramatic declines in their fish stocks, reducing a major source of food for some 60 million people. In the United States, the Colorado River, which has been diverted to irrigate crops in California, no longer reaches the sea. In China, the once mighty Yellow and Ganges rivers no longer flow because of excessive irrigation demands.

Land, a critical linchpin in supplying the world's food, is also becoming scarce. According to the FAO's recent report, *State of the World's Forests 2007*, between 1990 and 2005 the world lost 3 per cent of its total forests, a rate of approximately 0.2 per cent a year. Disappearing forests have a direct impact not only on the species that live there, but the loss of ecologically fragile forests also affects topsoil erosion. It can take between two hundred and a thousand years to grow 2.5 centimetres of rich topsoil, but in some parts of the world, erosion of topsoil is occurring in just sixteen years—a rate seventeen times faster than it can be replaced. Some 40 per cent of the world's agricultural land is also seriously degraded. In Central America, almost 75 per cent of the land is infertile. Credit Suisse estimates that, since the early 1960s, food production has been growing at a compound rate of 2.1 per cent a year, whereas the amount of arable land in the world is increasing at just 0.2 per cent—the difference between the two putting a serious constraint on our ability to meet the world's food needs.

FOOD AS FUEL

High oil prices and growing concern over the environment have prompted lawmakers around the world to pass legislation mandating the use of biofuels. In 2007, the U.S. Congress passed the Energy Independence and Security Act, aimed at increasing fuel economy in vehicles and promoting the use of alternative fuels. The law mandates that by 2022, 36 billion gallons of biofuels—or fuels made from food—be added to the nation's gasoline. In the U.S., the biofuel of choice is ethanol, a form of grain alcohol made from corn. When mixed with gasoline, ethanol acts as a fuel replacement or gasoline "extender" by reducing the carbon monoxide that cars produce. To pay for the program, Washington provides ethanol blenders with a subsidy of fifty-one cents a gallon while slapping a tariff of fifty-four cents a gallon on imported biofuels. It may seem like a good idea at first glance, but increasing demands for biofuels have been blamed for boosting the cost of food and, in the process, making it more difficult to feed the urban poor.

The debate over ethanol as a fuel additive has raged on since the Energy Independence and Security Act was passed into law. Detractors point to a surge in corn prices and the diversion of 20 per cent of the corn crop toward ethanol production, while supporters point to the need to reduce emissions. Others have focused on the inefficiency inherent in the conversion process. A study conducted by Cornell University in 2005 found that it took 29 per cent more energy to convert corn into ethanol than the fuel actually produced.[11]

Globally, the demand for biofuels has increased demand for grains by 100 million tons annually, or roughly 4.7 per cent of total grain production.[12] But these figures underestimate the true impact of America's ethanol program, in part because American farmers disproportionately produce some 42 per cent of the world's corn.[13] According to the IMF, corn ethanol production in the United States was responsible for at least half the rise in corn demand from 2005 to 2007. And with corn prices soaring from 2006 to 2008, U.S. farmers rotated their crops to produce more corn to cash in on the boom, driving the prices of soybeans and other crops higher on the way.

Repealing this act would send corn prices lower, but don't count on it happening any time soon given the Obama administration's solid commitment to environmental causes, and with corn and oil prices backing off their recent highs.

The most powerful lobby on Capitol Hill is the U.S. farm lobby. The industry benefits from a confusing set of disaster aid, counter-cyclical assistance and legacy payments that are provided for little or no output. Never mind that commercial farm households receive average annual incomes north of $85,000 a year and "farmers," such as well-known businessman David Rockefeller and talk show host David Letterman, receive subsidies to till the land.[14] So bizarre and conflicted is the situation in the U.S. that people can receive a subsidy to farm, even if it's not their principal occupation. All over the world, a byzantine system of regulations has been constructed to protect the domestic industry regardless of how foolhardy it may be.

OLD MACDONALD HAD A FARM

Two billion people in the world manage some 500 million small farms, each less than two hectares in size. These, in turn, support the approximately 3 billion people who live off the income that these small farms generate. In Africa, small-scale farming represents 80 per cent of all agricultural output. To meet the future needs of an expanding world, increasing the productivity of small farms will be a key consideration.

In developing countries, governments will need to focus their policies on structural changes that will allow smaller farmers to produce more food. In China, policy-makers have succeeded in distributing land in a more equitable manner that has made small farmers feel like they have a stake in agricultural development. While Chinese farms still need to become more productive, one hurdle—control over the land—has been effectively put to bed. If policies and key infrastructure such as roads and water systems aren't developed to aid these small farmers, however, a greater marginalization of the rural poor will occur and migration to urban areas will continue.

Credit Suisse believes the most obvious and straightforward solution to meeting surging global demand is increased farm commercialization—or a shift toward more sophisticated and larger-scale farming methods running along the food chain from seed to fertilizer companies to farms and on to the supermarket. In the 1930s, family farms were the norm in North America, but during the 1960s, greater competition allowed entrepreneurial farmers and corporations to consolidate the industry. Today, large-scale farms with size greater than eight hundred acres account for 60 per cent of agricultural production in the United States.[15] Achieving greater sophistication in farming practices will necessitate a number of fundamental changes to the industry globally. First, farmers must have control over the land that they work on, either through ownership or long-term leases; sufficient infrastructure must be in place to ensure that food can get to the market and crops can be irrigated; a system of checks and balances, as well as product standards, is needed to help farmers grow crops that meet acceptable global standards; and lastly, there must be ready access to capital so that farmers can obtain credit when they need it to buy seed, fertilizers or farm equipment.

The state of farm commercialization varies widely across the globe, but the most significant factor determining how quickly it occurs is the ease with which private money is allowed to flow toward agriculture. Europe, for example, has a long history of subsidies and other anti-competitive measures that keep people working but limit the economic output of the local farmers. Greater efficiency in farming will mean fewer farmers—a major issue in developing countries where farmers form a large percentage of the workforce. Finding work for these displaced farmers will be a key challenge as countries shift their agricultural practices from smaller subsistence farms to larger, more commercial operations.

In Argentina and Brazil, the process of farm commercialization is already well underway with a strong flow of private investment dollars to the agricultural sector. In Eastern Europe, Mexico and many countries in Southeast Asia, the process is still in its infancy, the limiting factor being issues of land transfer and ownership. Pakistan, India and Africa face challenges surrounding infrastructure and labour, while China must redistribute its workforce, 60 per cent of which are farmers. Yet, in spite of the challenges, Credit Suisse is forecasting that between now and 2015, demand for fertilizers and farm equipment will skyrocket as Russia, China, Eastern Europe and parts of Southeast Asia move toward greater farm commercialization.

In many developed countries, smaller farms are springing up based on the tenets of sustainable agriculture that embrace farm management over technology. These farms use older methods, such as crop rotation and the use of animal or other forms of "green" manure, instead of commercial fertilizers, to feed the soil and shun pesticides in favour of encouraging beneficial insects that aid in the production of crops. While sustainable agriculture will never offer the large-scale production necessary to close the widening gap between supply and demand for food, a growing chorus of consumers is nevertheless demanding the organic foods many of these farms produce and they are willing to pay a hefty premium for them.

CASHING IN ON CROPS

Farm commercialization will be the big driver in global agriculture over the next twenty years. As farms become more efficient, one obvious beneficiary will be the companies that make the tractors, combines, nutrient applicators and sprayers they need. Deere and Company, a global leader in farm equipment, was founded in 1837 and today boasts more than fifty-two thousand employees around the world. Case New Holland (CNH) is the other leading global supplier of farm equipment, with more than twenty-eight thousand employees in 160 countries. Beyond the solid fundamentals shored up by the growing demand for farm equipment, however, these companies have something else going for them: tremendous brand loyalty with many farmers identifying themselves as being either red (CNH) or green (John Deere). In most instances, the loyalty extends for generations.

Demand for the commercial fertilizer widely used in North America to dramatically increase crop yields will soar once the world recovers from the global financial crisis. Commercially fertilized fields grow 30 to 50 per cent faster than unfertilized fields, allowing farmers to boost their incomes substantially.

There are a wide variety of commercial chemical fertilizers that farmers use to meet the specific conditions of their soil and crops, all of which originate from three basic building blocks: nitrogen, phosphates and potash. Each nutrient plays a unique role in crop development, with specific soil conditions and the type of crop determining when and how much of each is required to obtain optimum yields. Nitrogen-based fertilizers are used in 59 per cent of all applications, phosphate-based fertilizers in 24 per cent and potash 17 per cent of the time.

Nitrogen-based fertilizers are made in plants around the world by converting natural gas, steam and pressure plus another substance to produce a wide variety of end products. Phosphate-based fertilizer comes from phosphate rock, which is crushed and mixed with water and sulphuric acid to form phosphoric acid. Potassium fertilizers come from potash mines, which at one time were underground salt lakes. While nitrogen is the dominant fertilizer worldwide, the business of producing nitrogen is highly fragmented and very competitive. By contrast, potassium-based fertilizers are produced in forty countries but, to be competitive, require ready access to phosphate rock. Two regions of the world are the dominant suppliers of phosphate rock for the potassium-based fertilizer business: Florida and Morocco.

Potash has the best industry dynamics of the three major nutrients since there are just twelve countries capable of producing potassium-based fertilizers. Canada controls 39 per cent of the global potash market through three major corporations, all with operations in Saskatchewan: PotashCorp, Agrium and Mosaic. The three also have banded together to form a marketing arm called Campotex that negotiates off-shore sales. Russia, another major producer, is home to Uralkali and Silvinit, which control an additional 23 per cent of global potash supply. So concentrated is the global potash industry that just seven companies, producing from twelve countries, control 85 per cent of global potash stocks.[16]

Saskatchewan boasts excellent infrastructure as well as a mature resource basin with few geological faults, qualities that make it extremely easy to mine and produce competitively. In addition to having lots of available land, Saskatchewan also has a well-qualified and knowledgeable workforce to develop the resource. As the most dominant potash basin in the world, Saskatchewan, along with its potash-producing companies, will grow rich with surging global demand for food.

PotashCorp is, in fact, the world's largest fertilizer enterprise. Although it produces all three primary plant nutrients—potash, nitrogen and phosphate—it is dominance in potash that helped make PotashCorp the most valuable company on the Toronto Stock Exchange in April 2008. The company has a 75 per cent share of all unused potash capacity in the province and a thousand-plus reserve life of potash resource.

Agrium is a major retailer of all three nutrients and a major supplier of controlled-release fertilizers. So attractive are the margins for producing potash in Saskatchewan that major mining companies such as BHP Billiton, the largest mining company in the world, and Rio Tinto have been scouting the province for acquisitions or raw land for their own projects.

China is the world's top consumer of fertilizers, followed by India, the U.S., Brazil and Russia. These five alone account for 67 per cent of total global demand. Although the amount of arable land globally is relatively static, having only increased by two-tenths of a per cent between 1961 and 2005, food production nevertheless increased by more than 2 per cent during this time frame, thanks to more effective fertilization of available land and increased farm commercialization.

FRANKENSEEDS

The biggest game changer for farmers over the next fifteen years, however, will be the use of genetically modified seeds. While fertilizers are crucial for boosting yields, genetically modified seeds offer a completely new competitive dynamic. "Genetically modified" (GM) is a general term that applies to any organism whose genetic material has been altered in a laboratory by recombining its DNA. The idea behind the process is to produce a seed or a plant that combines the

184

most desirable traits—everything from disease resistance to increased nutritional value.

Proponents of GM seeds and genetically modified organisms (GMOs) claim that they represent the only viable way of boosting production. Already, these products are meeting with huge commercial success in Argentina, Brazil, China, India and, of course, the U.S. The market for agricultural biotechnology has grown from approximately $3.1 billion in 2001 to more than $6 billion in 2006 and is expected to reach more than $8 billon by 2011. According to America's Monsanto, the global leader in GM seeds, the yield on American maize has doubled since 1970 with the use of fertilizers, and with genetically modified seeds it should double again by 2030.[17] But beyond their ability to increase farmers' yields, GM seeds also hold the promise of reducing the use of pesticides and commercial fertilizers, all of which could mean big bucks for farmers.

The detractors of these so-called Frankenfoods believe that the risks are just too great to accept their widespread use. They believe that so far, the impact on human health is unproven, and that by transferring genes across species we are entering a realm of unexpected biological consequences. The BBC reported that genetically modified crops can endure in the soil for at least ten years despite intensive efforts to eradicate them.[18] The European Union has come out solidly against the use of GM seeds and has not approved any since 1998.[19]

But GM seeds have made substantial inroads in America, where they are used to grow most of the country's corn crop. Pressure is mounting on the European Union to drop its resistance to these products, with companies such as Syngenta AG of Switzerland and Monsanto Company of St. Louis, Missouri, leading the charge for open competition within the European Union. In 2008, the *Financial Times* of London reported Peter Brabeck, the chairman of Nestlé SA as saying, "You cannot feed the world today without genetically modified organisms." When I met with the chief technology officer of Monsanto,

Robert Fraley, in Toronto during the fall of 2008, he made it quite clear that Europe would ultimately be forced by competitive pressures to drop its opposition to GM seeds or risk becoming a serious laggard in global agricultural production.

THE FOOD CHAIN

Higher food prices don't just affect the world's poor, they also pinch the margins at the food processing companies. Higher prices for wheat, corn and hogs particularly affect the makers of generic products, such as Cott Corporation, one of the world's largest non-alcoholic beverage companies, which are notorious for having skinny profits. Food is generally considered a recession-resistant business—given that eating isn't optional—and for the average European and North American it still represents only about 10 per cent of overall expenses, making price hikes less of a big deal.

When food prices moved higher, Western consumers reacted by altering what they ate, where they ate and where they bought their groceries. McDonald's restaurants has seen an enormous resurgence in its business, while Whole Foods Markets, a Texas-based specialty grocer focused on organic and fancier foods, has seen both its business and its share price slump. The food processing companies in the best position to weather the storm are the *multinationals*: companies such as Nestlé, Danone and Unilever—all of which have the diversity of markets and the scale to buy in bulk and thus keep their prices as low as possible until the food fight subsides.

Investors can profit from the increasing focus on all things agricultural by buying the shares of companies that produce the fertilizers, seeds and tractors that farmers around the globe will soon need. Specialty chemical manufacturers that produce things like pesticides and herbicides will likely see volume increases in the years to come, but as GM seeds make more of an inroad into their traditional markets, there will be pressure on these companies to evolve. The agricultural sector well may be the best bet for investors among all commodity-oriented sectors, as it is largely insensitive to economic pressures. A growing global population, competition from biofuels and the fact that eating is a necessity of life make investing in agricultural stocks a good way to grow your portfolio.

Fertilizer stocks, in particular, offer investors huge upside potential. Historically low grain stocks, changing diets and no economic alternatives position fertilizers for a strong rebound when the global economy begins to recover. While the jury is out on genetically modified seeds and the decision to purchase a tractor can be postponed, farmers can't maximize their yields if for more than two years in a row they skip applying the critical nutrients that their soil needs. But, like all commodity stocks, fertilizer stocks are susceptible to booms and busts. The timing has rarely been this attractive to spread some fertilizer stocks into your portfolio as the world has never needed modern approaches to farming more.

CHAPTER SUMMARY

- Exploding demand and static supply mean food inflation is here to stay.
- Limits to arable land, demand for biofuels, surging global population and changing diets are underpinning higher prices.
- Fertilizer companies, particularly potash suppliers, will benefit from food inflation.
- Farm equipment manufacturers will benefit from a global trend toward mass farm commercialization.
- GM seeds, while controversial, could be a game-changer for farmers and investors.
- Inroads made by GM seed manufacturers will be at the expense of pesticide and herbicide producers.

13

CANADA INNOVATES

As Canadians, we tend to be our own harshest critics, particularly when it comes to our role as a player in the global economy. But is the criticism justified? Absolutely not. Canada excels at far more than just having resources; we have leading companies in technology, media, manufacturing and consumer products. We boast a highly educated workforce and emerging knowledge and technology hubs that have already spawned global businesses. As far as nationhood goes, Canada is still the new kid on the block, which makes our accomplishments even more remarkable. The long-term economic future for Canada will be in technology and in knowledge-based businesses. Contrary to what you've heard from the naysayers, our cultural diversity, cutting-edge research institutions, educated population and free-market economy will make us ideally positioned for the twenty-first century and beyond.

THINKING *INSIDE* THE BOX

Waterloo's Research In Motion (RIM) and its iconic BlackBerry could not have hoped for a better pitchman than U.S. president Barack Obama. Told he would have to lose the device after he took the oath of office, Obama campaigned hard to keep it, and won a partial victory. He, like millions of users all over the world, has admitted his addiction to the wireless handheld device—dubbed the "Crackberry" by some—that puts all the services users want right inside the box. With its innovative "push" technology that forwards emails to the device in real time and synchronizes instantly with its owner's PC back at the office, the BlackBerry has become the global leader in so-called smart phones. No other device-maker has been able to duplicate RIM's proprietary network with high-encryption security that has made its products such a hit with corporate clients. Creative thinking at RIM has made the BlackBerry sleeker, smaller and incredibly versatile, and has cemented the company's stranglehold on the corporate mobile computing market. By offering mobile access to email, a phone, calendar functions, contact lists, a camera, the Internet and Internet-based applications, BlackBerry has become the must-have device for busy corporate types. The more recent versions have the added functionality of allowing users to open PowerPoint and PDF attachments and edit Word and Excel files. The superior functionality of the BlackBerry has allowed RIM to capture an enviable 77 per cent share of the corporate market for mobile handheld devices.[1]

RIM was founded in 1984 by two engineering students, Mike Lazaridis and his friend Douglas Fregin. Lazaridis and his family immigrated to Canada from Istanbul, Turkey, in 1966, and settled in Windsor, Ontario. From an early age, Lazaridis was fascinated by how things work and spent his childhood building radios and rockets. At age twelve, he won a prize for reading every science book in the Windsor Public Library and in 1979 he enrolled in electrical engineering at the University of Waterloo. While at Waterloo, Lazaridis and Fregin founded RIM, which was originally a computer science and electronics consulting business. Just two months before Lazaridis was to graduate from Waterloo, General Motors offered RIM a $600,000 contract. Lazaridis dropped out of school to concentrate on building RIM, with a new focus on wireless data transmission and wireless point-of-sale customer terminals.

In 1992, Jim Balsillie, a Harvard MBA, joined RIM and injected $250,000 of his own money into the company. With Balsillie's business acumen and Lazaridis's technical know-how, RIM expanded from a small company of fewer than ten employees in 1992 to a company with more than 8,100 employees and sales of more than $4.9 billion in 2007. In the process, the company became a stock market darling and made billionaires out of Balsillie and Lazaridis. But it did more than that. It also proved wrong the conventional wisdom that Canada's market was just too small to support a viable branded consumer products business.

OUTSIDE-THE-BOX THINKING

Lazaridis's enormous success with RIM has allowed him to pursue one of his other loves—the advancement of physics. The Perimeter Institute of Theoretical Physics (PI) was founded in 1999 as an independent institution dedicated to pure research in the foundations of quantum physics. The brainchild of Lazaridis, PI was established in Waterloo, just down the street from RIM's headquarters. In 2000, the Lazaradis family donated $100 million to the institute, and operations began the following year under the leadership of a core of nine world-class physicists. In June 2008, Lazaridis donated a further $50 million to Perimeter. Lazaridis was quoted in *Wired* magazine saying he believes that if scientists can figure out how to unify the forces of nature, great change will happen. For example, the telephone, phonograph and cell phone were all brought about through the unification of electricity and magnetism.[2]

In creating PI, Lazaridis might just have revolutionized the way pure research is conducted in Canada. As an independent institute, PI rejects the bureaucratic model all too familiar in most university settings. The institute doesn't offer tenure, nor does it require researchers to teach classes or mark term papers. People are recruited to PI to *think*. The sixty-five-thousand-square-foot complex is replete with a squash court, bistro and 205-seat auditorium. Coffee is free. The bistro, the Black Hole, often hosts dinners complete with baroque and jazz music. The institute pays top dollar to get the best researchers on the planet, who, in turn, attract other bright minds eager for a chance to work under the wide latitude they are given.

The *who's who* list at the institute seems to grow by the day. In November 2008 it was announced that renowned physicist Stephen Hawking was to become a Distinguished Research Chair there the following year. Health problems prevented Hawking from taking up the post, however, the roster of leading physicists continues to grow. Xiao-Gang Wen, a physics professor from MIT; Raymond Laflamme, an information theorist from Los Alamos National Lab; and Neta Bahcall, a professor of astrophysics from Princeton, all came to Waterloo over the past five years.[3] The hoped-for quantum breakthrough has so far eluded PI, but the sense that it is on the cusp of something great is a driving force for the institute. Already, PI ranks as one of the best among only a handful of theoretical physics institutions worldwide.

THE NEXUS

The University of Waterloo and its surrounding region form an important knowledge nexus within Canada. Founded by local industrialists and championed by Dr. Gerald Hagey, a former sales manager for local rubber company B.F. Goodrich, the university was founded in 1957. As its first president, Hagey recognized that Canada needed more graduates in the sciences and believed the co-operative education model would give Waterloo an edge over other universities. His instincts proved bang on. The university's focus on math and science, with students and faculty regularly partnering with industry, was a radical departure from the typical arts and science programs offered at colleges and universities around the world. Since its founding, the university has gone on to become Canada's third largest, with its partnership with the private sector being an essential part of its appeal.

With more than thirteen thousand students enrolled in co-op programs that alternate work and school terms, the university has actually become the largest provider of co-operative education in the world. If imitation is the sincerest form of flattery, then the University of Waterloo should feel very flattered indeed—its blueprint has now spread to more than one hundred colleges and universities across Canada.[4] It also boasts the largest mathematics faculty in the world, with more than 5,300 students and 200 full-time professors teaching over 180 courses in math and computer science.[5]

Computer science is another area at which Waterloo excels—even from its early days. Dr. Douglas Wright, Waterloo's president from 1981 to 1993, recalls that "many times we would have the processor in the lab before the company introduced it into the market. IBM Canada once credited Waterloo co-ops for establishing computers with small and medium-sized businesses across the country."[6] Waterloo's preeminence in the sciences has won the respect of Bill Gates, founder of Microsoft, and one of the richest men in the world. In October 2005, Gates told *CTV News*, "Waterloo is a very special relationship for us," adding, "Most years, we hire more students out of Waterloo than any university in the world, typically 50 or even more."[7]

Over the years, Waterloo has fostered more than 275 "spinoffs"— companies that collectively generate over $1 billion in annual revenue.[8] A notable example is Open Text Corporation, the world's largest independent provider of Enterprise Content Management (ECM) software. Today, the company supports more than forty-six thousand customers in twelve languages in 114 countries and has annual revenues of about $1 billion, a healthy level for a software firm. The company evolved from a University of Waterloo project whose aim was to provide string-search technology and full-text indexing for the *Oxford English Dictionary*.[9]

VeloCity, a unique tool aimed at fostering innovation, was the brain-child of another University of Waterloo staffer, Sean Van Koughnett. The question that gave rise to VeloCity was simple: what would happen if you filled a whole university dorm with graduate and upper-year students and gave them the latest gadgets and tools for collaboration? Waterloo is bet-ting that the next Google could spring from a creative and collaborative living arrangement like VeloCity. After all, some of the most successful technology companies in the world have started with a lot less.[10]

SPRECHEN ZIE INSURANCE

The original German immigrants who settled the Kitchener-Waterloo area were cautious and conservative people who believed in commu-nity co-operation. None espoused this ideal more than the Mennonites, however, a Protestant religious group that shuns most modern conve-niences, including cars and electricity. There is thus some irony to the fact that it was the Mennonites that helped spawn Waterloo's mutual insurance companies in the late nineteenth and twentieth centuries. Mutual Life Assurance Company, founded in 1868, grew to become national in scope and was eventually acquired in 2002 by Sun Life Financial. Equitable Life is based in the area and so too is Manulife Financial, which employs four thousand people locally. As a result, the Kitchener-Waterloo region has become the mecca for insurance in-dustry talent and puts twelve thousand people to work in the process.[11]

GET GROWING

A little closer to Toronto is Guelph, Ontario, whose university is a rec-ognized global leader in all things agricultural. With food becoming a hot button issue, the research carried out by the University of Guelph will become increasingly valuable. In October 2008, it opened two new research facilities dedicated to the agricultural sciences. The first, the Bioproducts Discovery & Development Centre, is looking into the pos-sibility of turning crops such as soy and corn into fuel, resins, plastics or just about anything you can imagine. The concept behind the centre is to create environmentally sustainable alternatives that can benefit the economy and the farmer at the same time. The other new research facility is the Centre for Agricultural Renewable Energy and Sustainability, whose focus is on leveraging training and research to strengthen the agricultural sector.[12]

The University of Guelph has also put itself on the cutting edge of animal science with its trademarked "Enviropigs." With their squealing and grunting, Enviropigs look like ordinary oinkers to the average observer, but they aren't; they have been genetically modified by university researchers to provide a healthier source of pork in what is potentially a new era of food production. While transgenic meats are somewhat controversial, the Food and Drug Administration (FDA) in the U.S. has already given the green light to food products made from them. The first Enviropig was born in 1999, adapted from mouse DNA that allowed it to produce a bacterial protein called phytase gene. This gene allowed the pig to digest the phosphorus found in plants more efficiently—reducing the phosphorus in their waste by up to 60 per cent. Less phosphorus in pig waste means less leaching of it from pig manure into the lakes and streams where it can kill fish. While it remains to be seen if the Enviropig will gain acceptance in the U.S., the possibility that these transgenic meats may be coming to your dinner plate sometime soon offers intriguing possibilities for investors. Prior to the FDA's guidelines, food companies were slow to back these genetically modified animals without a clear approval process. The approval has changed all of that, opening the door for investors to participate in Guelph's trademarked pig.[13]

Researchers at Guelph are not just limiting themselves to the study of earthly agriculture, however. A team of approximately sixty-five faculty, students and staff are working at a state-of-the-art research facility that has turned Canada into a leader in the world of "space agriculture." Up until now, one limitation to space travel was the food required for sustaining long-term exploration. A possible solution, which researchers at Guelph are working on, is growing plants in space in order to support human life. Mike Dixon, the director of the Controlled Environment Systems Research Facility at the university, was quoted in the *Montreal Gazette* declaring, "We want to grow the first plant on the moon." He went on to say, "Let's face it, the next worse place after a snowbank in Canada to do controlled-environmental plant production has got to be the moon."[14]

AROUND THE HILL

The greater Ottawa region has consistently been a breeding ground for high-tech innovation. Ottawa-based Bell-Northern Research (BNR) was, at one time, one of the best telecommunications research and development organizations in the world. The firm boasted campuses around the world and was responsible for many pioneering achievements with the telephone. During the 1970s, BNR championed the concept of the telephone switch as a computer rather than as a mechanical piece of hardware, which allowed for the development of features such as conferencing and call forwarding. In 1975, the company introduced the Meridian SL-1, a highly successful line of business phones incorporating this new digital capability aimed at mid-sized businesses. Bob Gaskins, a researcher based in the U.S., was responsible for inventing PowerPoint, the popular presentation software, when he worked at BNR.[15]

For much of its history, BNR was jointly owned by Bell Canada and Northern Telecom. During the 1990s, BNR was gradually absorbed into Northern Telecom, which by 1998, with the acquisition of Bay Networks, had changed its name to Nortel Networks Corporation, or Nortel. Alumni from Nortel have gone on to form their own companies and further develop the region and Canada's information technology industry. The *Globe and Mail* cites figures from the Information Technology Association of Canada (ITAC) that peg the number of existing firms at 260; others believe that there are at least 450 firms in the Ottawa region alone.[16] The jobs created in information technology tend to be good ones, with salaries averaging $58,600 in 2007. As such, they attract highly skilled workers, some 43 per cent of which have a university degree, according to ITAC. Canada's cadre of information technology workers numbers around six hundred thousand—more than are employed in our auto sector.

During the late 1990s, Nortel's stock hit the stratosphere as the market hoped that the firm's sales of network gear would reap increasing profits. At its peak market valuation, Nortel accounted for more than a third of the total valuation of the Toronto Stock Exchange. As recently as 2007, Nortel was spending $1.8 billion a year on research and development, making it a Canadian leader in technology spending. But a series of missteps, an alleged accounting fraud and an inability to turn a profit eventually led to Nortel filing for bankruptcy protection from creditors in Canada, the U.S. and the U.K. on January 14, 2009.

Technologies rise and fall and successful companies need to constantly reinvent themselves. While the loss of Nortel, along with its ability to act as an incubator of fresh ideas and technologies, is indeed tragic, talented former employees may soon sow the seeds of tomorrow's next BNR.

MEDIA MOGUL, EH?

In media, Canada is also a global leader, boasting one of the world's largest and most influential media organizations. Thomson Corp.'s $19 billion acquisition of Reuters Group Limited in May 2007 catapulted the newly minted Thomson Reuters into the major leagues of the media world. With 25 million global subscribers spanning fields as diverse as law, accounting, tax, science, health care and financial services, Thomson Reuters is a global powerhouse. The firm combines industry expertise with technology to deliver critical information to decision-makers in a wide variety of fields. The 2008 *BusinessWeek* ranking of the top hundred global brands placed Thomson Reuters at number forty-four, just behind Philips, the Dutch electronics giant. With 2007 revenues of more than $12.4 billion, a presence in ninety-three countries and more than fifty thousand employees, Thompson Reuters is truly a giant of global media.[17]

Prior to the merger, Thomson Corporation had grown to global prominence through the steady leadership of Ken Thomson, who took over the helm after the passing of his father, Roy Thomson, also known as Baron Thomson of Fleet. The empire his father had built started from a single newspaper, the *Timmins Daily Press*, but by the time of the elder Thompson's death in 1976 it had evolved into an extensive collection of television and newspaper holdings, which Ken inherited along with the title Lord Thomson of Fleet. Although he was addressed as Lord Thomson when he visited London, in his down-to-earth style he preferred to be known simply as Ken. Over the course of its history, the Thomson Corporation held such prestigious newspapers as the *Globe and Mail* (Toronto), *Times* (London) and *Jerusalem Post* (Israel). Beginning in 2000, the company sold all of its newspapers and focused attention on becoming a world leader in financial data, information services and academic publishing.

Reuters was founded in 1851 by Paul Julius Reuters to provide stock quotes from London to Paris and vice versa using the newest technology of the day: the submarine telegraph system. The firm evolved from its beginnings as a provider of financial market data to become a global news service providing reports from around the world to television and newspapers.

The transformation of Thomson Reuters from a holding company of print newspapers to an electronic deliverer of focused workflow solutions for professionals has positioned the company for future success. Unlike traditional print or television businesses that are advertising-dependent, the electronic delivery solutions model of Thomson Reuters faces very few competitive threats and is also a more stable operating platform. The firm's most successful platform is in the legal segment, where it enjoys a dominant position. According to TD Newcrest, the legal segment "has rational competition, high barriers to entry, attractive organic revenue growth prospects, rising margins and stable capital expenditure requirements."[18] What's more, the same consolidation that occurred in the legal segment could occur in the financial services segment—a move that would make Thomson Reuters, along with privately held Bloomberg L.P., part of a duopoly in the electronic delivery of financial solutions for investment professionals. Thomson Reuters is a media empire for the twenty-first century, with stable revenues and the strong potential to grow market share and margins across a range of industries in the years to come.

FLYING HIGH

We're always hearing about the outsourcing of North American jobs to low-wage countries, but Bombardier of Montreal is bucking the trend. Formed in 1942 by a Quebec mechanic named Joseph-Armand Bombardier, the company's first product was a snowmobile. During the Second World War, it produced vehicles for the military and, later, all-terrain vehicles used in oil, forestry and mining. The company launched the popular Ski-Doo in 1959 and, overnight, a new winter sport was born in Quebec. Today, the company operates two main divisions, the transportation division being the largest manufacturer of rolling stock in the world, while the aerospace division builds regional aircraft and business jets. The firm is a Fortune Global 500 company, with 2008 revenues of US$17.5 billion.[19]

Bombardier's aerospace division is responsible for more than half the firm's revenues, generated by the families of aircraft it manufactures for both regional airlines and business clientele. For those with serious coin, Bombardier manufactures the Learjet, Challenger and Global series of business aircraft. While they aren't turning away too many billionaires with lofty ambitions these days, corporate largesse is definitely out of favour with the public. But while that hostility could spell trouble for the business jet division, many businesses are using their jets as *true* productivity enhancers. For example, Wal-Mart stores, the largest retailer in the world, uses its fleet of twenty-seven Bombardier jets to ferry executives around the world to check up on their stores and those of the competition. The typical Wal-Mart corporate jet makes somewhere between three and six stops a day, ferrying teams of five or more people to stores across the globe.[20]

Bombardier Aerospace also manufactures commercial aircraft designed for regional applications. The popular Q Series is a turboprop series of plane used by airlines such as Porter, based at Toronto's City Centre ("island") Airport, and offers flights to locations as far away as Halifax. The CRJ Series of jets is the most successful regional jet program in history, with more than 1,300 in service. The company recently embarked on creating the C Series of commercial aircraft—the only aircraft designed specifically for the 100- to 149-passenger capacity market. The C Series is being designed to offer full operational commonality, a reduced environmental footprint and a 15 per cent reduction in cash operating costs. The company expects to have the C Series fully developed and in service by 2013 and, by 2027, it hopes to have sold 6,300 aircraft. The aircraft business can experience turbulence from time to time, but with an order backlog of $26.1 billion in the middle of 2008, Bombardier still seems to be flying high.[21]

COME IN, GROUND CONTROL

In designing and building mission-critical applications and complex space systems, Canada punches well above its weight. MacDonald, Dettwiler and Associates (TSX: MDA) of Richmond, B.C., is a Canadian technology success story that is an industry leader in outer space, as well as here on Earth. Formed in 1969, MDA has become a diversified technology company, providing airborne surveillance systems, Earth observation ground systems and electronic information products. Today, the company operates from twenty-five offices throughout North America and the United Kingdom and employs more than 3,200 people worldwide. While the company earns most of its revenue from its Information Products division, the sexier part of the business is the advanced robotic systems that operate in hostile environments. With governments around the world growing increasingly concerned about defence and intelligence gathering, MDA has seen a steady stream of interest in its monitoring technologies. But the application that the company is best known for is the Canadarm, the robotic arm that is used to move payloads around in space.

The Information Products division of MDA delivers high-resolution satellite images and information products to the real estate industry. By collecting, digitizing and organizing real estate data into a service offering that saves time and effort, MDA has built a strong franchise. The services the division provides allows you to determine quickly what a property is worth based on recent assessments and whether or not there is a lien outstanding against the property. In British Columbia, the company operates an electronic service called BC OnLine, which allows customers to search for property assessments, liens, legal title and property tax information. In the U.S., the company provides residential and commercial property valuation services to the insurance and financial services industries and in the U.K., the company has entered into an exclusive arrangement with the U.K. government to operate the National Land and Property Information Service. While real estate values have fallen sharply in the U.S. and U.K., MDA's Information Products business has held up surprisingly well. Even with a real estate collapse in its major markets, the margins for its Information Products division have remained steady—an encouraging sign.

The company is pretty much the only game in town when it comes to Canadian space contractors. National Bank Financial estimates that in 2009, MDA will receive contracts worth around $190 million from the Canadian Space Agency (CSA) alone. With technological breakthroughs such as the Canadarm functioning flawlessly in space, the very real potential exists for MDA to commercialize some of its leading-edge technology. The Information Products division has just weathered a perfect storm in the global real estate market, coming through the maelstrom in good shape. With a diverse range of service offerings and clients, MDA is one Canadian technology giant that is dominant both on land and in space.[22]

BUCKLE UP

While most airlines are busy racking up losses faster than most of us are accumulating Air Miles, Calgary's WestJet Airlines is gobbling up market share as its competitors falter. A potent combination of a smart operating strategy, a lack of legacy issues and a high-performance culture has contributed to WestJet's runaway success. Business has been up, up and away for WestJet ever since it began service with just three jets in 1996. Today, the airline's fleet has grown to seventy-six new-generation Boeing 737s. But what has made WestJet a success is the WestJet experience. The airline boasts North America's youngest fleet, a younger labour force and an attitude that truly says *welcome aboard*. On WestJet, there is no first class seating. Everyone is treated the same—with friendly air crews, plush leather seating and real-time television shows you can watch while in the air. The WestJet experience is simply better.

Behind the superior experience is a superior operating strategy, one that involves a relentless focus on cutting costs while not cutting down the experience of flying WestJet. From the beginning, the airline selected the Boeing 737 as the plane of choice. With just one model of aircraft, flight training is simplified, flight crews are streamlined and maintenance is more straightforward. In short, money is saved.

But the real genius was in making WestJet employees owners of the company. Today, eighty-four per cent of the employee base participates in the company's share purchase plan and profit-sharing program. That has kept out the unions and helped foster a culture of genuine caring, not only for the passengers but for the profitability of the airline. After all, when *you* are an owner, unnecessary costs and waste are ultimately coming out of *your* pocket.

Since 1996, the airline's results have been impressive. While most other airlines in North America are a sea of red ink, WestJet has been consistently profitable. While others are cutting back on routes, meals or service, WestJet has been growing market share at a clip of two or three per cent each and every year it's been in business. And that's translated into an impressive market share of the Canadian air travel market of thirty-seven per cent. But for Sean Durfy, the CEO of WestJet, a market share of forty-five to fifty per cent is where the company is aspiring to be by 2013. With a great team, a superior strategy and a passion for excellence, the sky is the limit to the business heights that WestJet can attain.[23]

GET CREATIVE

Dr. Richard Florida is an American academic who has studied and written extensively on prosperity and the role that creativity plays in fostering regional growth. Today, Florida lives in Toronto where he is a director of the Martin Prosperity Institute, Rotman School of Management at the University of Toronto. "What makes Toronto so transformative and exciting," wrote Florida in a 2008 edition of *Toronto Life* magazine, "is that it is uniquely situated—geographically and socially—to take advantage of the global transformation to a creative economy."[24] When Florida speaks about a "creative economy" he is referring to a knowledge-based economy where people are paid to *think*. Those who do the thinking are what he calls the "creative class," a category who includes artists, scientists, analysts and managers alike. Toronto is one of the ten largest mega-regions in the world, but also one of Canada's most open and tolerant cultures—qualities that make it ideally suited to foster the development of a creative class.

Ever since the 1950s, the proportion of working class people who use physical skills to do repetitive tasks, such as assembly line workers, has been declining, while the creative class has been growing. Today, 22 per cent of Canada's workforce is considered working class, while 34 per cent are now engaged in creative occupations. The bulk of our workforce, some 41 per cent, is composed of service workers such as clerks, waiters, janitors and transit workers, whose role is to support those engaged in the creative occupations. The transition to a creativity-based economy is important for many reasons, but primarily because of the "wealth effect" that a creative economy can bestow. According to Florida, creative occupations earn 39 per cent more on average than all other categories of workers. Not only that, but the creative class does much better when times are tough, the rate of unemployment among its members having been a third of that of the working class since 1998. So by fostering your creative talents, you get paid more and are more likely to keep working in a difficult economic environment.[25]

The economic future belongs to the people and nations that will emphasize the type of knowledge-based work Florida describes. To prosper in the twenty-first century, Canada needs to foster a more idea-based economy and to adequately reward people for their creative contributions. In so doing, we will produce more champions, such as RIM, that offer a dramatically superior business and consumer product that customers are prepared to pay a premium for. In 2008, Ontario premier Dalton McGuinty commissioned Dr. Florida and Roger Martin, dean of the University of Toronto's Rotman School of Business, to write a report on Ontario's competitiveness. The academics found that Ontario needs to speed the transition to an economy based on brainpower by encouraging more residents to attend college or university and by improving the connectivity between urban centres.[26]

Canada is also a world leader when it comes to education. According to the Paris-based OECD, which analyzes and forecasts economic and social data, in 2006 Canada and Ontario ranked among the leaders globally in a wide variety of educational categories, including reading and science. Canadians also appear to be more literate than Americans. Only 13 per cent of Canadians identify themselves as non-readers versus a whopping 43 per cent of Americans who fall into that category.[27] The OECD also notes that social mobility in Canada is better than in most other countries, meaning that poor children stand a reasonably good chance of becoming rich, and vice versa.[28] In tomorrow's ideas-based world, having an education will be a key success factor in attaining the good life.

Excellent cell phone networks and access are another essential tool for knowledge workers in our increasingly mobile and interconnected world. Canada's mobile phone usage, measured in air-time minutes, is the second-highest in the world.* Only in America do people talk for longer when cell phone usage is measured on an average minutes-per-use basis. Internet penetration rates in Canada are also among the highest in the world. Nearly 84 per cent of Canadian homes have Internet access, versus only 75 per cent in the U.S.[29] According to Internet World Stats, an international website featuring up-to-date world Internet usage, Canada is also a world leader in e-commerce.[30] In a world where access to information and knowledge is crucial, Canada's ability to connect globally via the Internet will position us well for the future.

Canada has the educational institutions, culture, social mobility and telecommunications infrastructure to be a serious competitor in the global economy. The future will belong to societies that are open, idea-based and interconnected—in short, places like Canada.

---

*In making this comparison, I have multiplied handset penetration by average minutes of use. The reason I chose this metric is that handset penetration numbers alone don't discriminate between prepaid and postpaid mobile phone revenue. In many countries of the world, low-value prepaid services dominate the market and therefore skew the penetration data unfairly toward those countries.

CHAPTER SUMMARY

- Everything you've heard about Canada's economic shortcomings just isn't true.
- BlackBerry-maker Research In Motion offers proof that Canada can develop and grow successful global consumer products.
- The Kitchener-Waterloo and Guelph regions form a knowledge nexus that will spawn the next generation of high-tech, agricultural and environmental companies.
- The Ottawa region is a technology hub.
- Bombardier proves that Canada can engineer and manufacture transportation solutions at a world-class level.
- Canada's Thompson Reuters is a global media giant.
- Canada has one of the highest per capita rates of high-speed Internet use and mobile telephony.

14

VERTIGO

The global financial crisis has left most of us frightened. Our savings have been destroyed and our confidence in the markets has been shattered. In the blink of an eye, the U.S. subprime housing crisis morphed, seemingly overnight, into a global banking and economic meltdown. Around the world, the story is much the same—it all happened so quickly. Investors have lost anywhere from a quarter to a third of their savings. To compensate, they will need to cut back on their spending, which will exacerbate the situation in the real economy. In an interconnected, globalized world, the problems are more complex and so too are the solutions. Investors are dazed and confused and uncertain about the future. Many financial experts have called for a quick recovery from "oversold" levels, but don't bet on it.

As the crisis drags on and hope over yet *another* stimulus package begins to wane, consumer confidence is slumping. A global poll on the subject taken in January 2009 showed that 49 per cent of respondents believed the situation would worsen in the next three months.[1] In a world where 60 per cent of the world's economy can be tied to consumer spending, weak confidence readings spell trouble.

California is struggling to pay down debt. Its chief accountant, John Chiang, warned in January 2009 that the state would need to postpone payments, including welfare cheques, income tax refunds totalling nearly $2 billion, and student grants, to avoid running out of cash. While the measures are expected to be temporary, Chiang has already indicated that more deferrals are possible. A budget impasse and a municipal bond market that has seized up, particularly for states with weak credit ratings, have also contributed to California's predicament. In December 2008, the state's governor, Arnold Schwarzenegger, ordered some state employees to take two days off a month—a move aimed at saving the state $1.4 billion over seventeen months and helping to close the budget gap.[2] Once an economic powerhouse, California is now struggling and might become technically insolvent in the near future.

BUNGLING BANKERS

A job on Wall Street, once a coveted prize, has become an object of ridicule. Online vendors selling "I Hate Investment Banking" T-shirts have sprung up.[3] John Thain, the former Chief Executive Officer at Merrill Lynch, was forced out of Bank of America in January 2009, after it was revealed that large bonuses were paid to Merrill staffers even after Bank of America received additional government funds, in late 2008, to help complete the merger with Merrill to save it from certain bankruptcy. Adding fuel to the fire, it was revealed that Thain had spent $1.2 million to redecorate his new office at Bank of America, $68,000 of which was shelled out for a credenza and $87,000 for a rug.[4] The next month, America's top bankers were hauled in front of Congress and the general public to face the heat from lawmakers over their lavish spending of taxpayers' money. Treated like errant schoolchildren, the banking bigwigs were forced to raise their hands in response to blanket questions about their expenditures and any changes they might have implemented since this crisis began. The bankers pledged to regain the public's trust—a tall order.[5]

As the accountants tally up the cost of a party that went on for far too long, one thing seems assured: global banking will need to shrink. As the house of cards grew taller, America's banking industry's share of *total* corporate profits soared to more than 40 per cent in 2007 from approximately 10 per cent in 1980, while at the same time, its share of the stock market's value ran to 23 per cent from 6 per cent. Yet in spite of their seeming importance, America's banks only employed 5 per cent of the private sector.[6] Were these banks really creating sufficient value to justify the share prices they were getting? No.

MAELSTROM

In January 2009, Iceland's conservative government was forced from power as protests mounted in the streets of this tiny nation. Iceland's currency collapsed in October 2008, leaving many Icelanders unable to pay their debts.[7] In Spain, the unemployment rate hit 14 per cent in January 2009, an increase of 47 per cent from the prior year, and it might reach as high as 20 per cent by 2011. The government has even taken the drastic step of paying foreign workers residing in Spain not to compete for jobs that native Spaniards could fill.[8] There are at least eight hundred thousand unsold homes on the Spanish property market and the recession is the worst in fifty years.[9] France's economy, likewise, has already shrunk more than at any time in the last three decades. In Britain, striking nuclear and coal-fired electricity plant workers held signs saying "Put British workers first." In eastern and central Europe the situation is even worse, as local banks relied heavily on a flood of foreign capital during the boom years in order to finance their rapid expansion. Now with a full-blown crisis underway, foreigners are yanking home their capital, causing the currencies of these countries to plunge and unemployment to soar. All across Europe, protests and strikes are growing as workers fight for the few remaining jobs.[10]

The economic stresses between the individual member countries of the European Union may even threaten the very existence of the monetary union. A single national currency and central bank can respond to a crisis by slashing interest rates dramatically to stimulate growth or by devaluing the currency. Despite its widely divergent economies, however, the European Central Bank can only implement a one-size-fits-all monetary policy for the sixteen-member block, even in times like this. Countries such as Spain, Greece and Ireland, where economic conditions are dire, will be tempted to bail out their domestic economies with government spending. But that could well throw them offside with the European Union's mandate of a maximum government deficit of 3 per cent of GDP. The union will likely hold, but as long as talk of dissolution persists, the euro will come under pressure.

Global political destabilization is another possible consequence of the meltdown. In February 2009, U.S. intelligence agencies reported that the global economic crisis was *the* biggest U.S. security risk in the near term. In a briefing before Congress, Admiral Dennis Blair spoke of the anti-government protests in Europe and Russia. In another briefing to the Senate Intelligence Committee, Blair elaborated, saying, "Instability can loosen the fragile hold that many developing countries have on law and order, which can spill out in dangerous ways to the international community."[11]

NOT IN MY BACKYARD

In this worsening economy, it seems like everyone and his dog has gone searching for a bailout. In late 2008, the executives of the "big three" Detroit car companies flew on private jets to Washington to beg for help, where they received a knuckle-wrapping for their insensitivity. On their second visit, needless to say, they drove. European car-makers soon figured they, too, should receive a bailout if their competition was getting one.

A long lineup of workers, industry executives and private citizens is forming around the corridors of political power in capitals around the world, obliging governments to listen and, in many instances, to act. As

Barack Obama's initial stimulus package was winding its way through the Congress and then the Senate in early 2009, a "Buy American" clause was inserted into the draft legislation. The lawmakers' intent was clear: why spend U.S. taxpayer money on goods and services made outside the country? But protectionist measures such as Buy American are a slippery slope that could set off tit-for-tat retaliatory trade wars, with every country scrambling to one-up the other by hiding behind protective trade barriers. While the most objectionable language in the bill was subsequently removed, the next time around politicians might not be so willing to acquiesce to external pressure. Trade wars never end well, tending instead to only prolong and deepen economic malaise.

The recent crisis wasn't the first time that lawmakers responded to the siren call of domestic interests. For politicians under pressure, blaming *foreigners* for everything that's wrong is par for the course. In 1930, against the urging of over a thousand economists, U.S. President Herbert Hoover signed into law the Smoot-Hawley Tariff Act, a trade-restricting law that caused global trade to decline by two-thirds between 1929 and 1934. Today, this piece of legislation is widely blamed for extending and deepening the Great Depression. The jury on the Obama administration is still out. Obama has shown a willingness to work with other world leaders, particularly Canada, but the Democrats in Congress have been leaning toward protectionist measures. Obama is on record, for example, saying that the North American Free Trade Agreement was "a big mistake."

When times are tough at home, protectionist sentiments and foreign-bashing can be a great way for politicians to pick up some votes in the short term. By limiting competition from abroad by imposing trade barriers, governments hope to save jobs. But in so doing, they turn back the clock on global trade and economic progress—forces that over the last three decades have lifted hundreds of millions of people around the world out of poverty. The investment thesis I have outlined in this book is dependent on the notion of open and continuing global trade.

Bilateral trade deals between nations and organizations such as the World Trade Organization make the return of a Smoot-Hawley world less likely. But investors should be mindful: politics is still politics.

AVOID THE DEEP END OF THE POOL

A rally in the stock market can be exciting, and it's often tempting to jump back in at the first signs of a recovery. But doing so is often foolish; the repercussions of financial crises tend to be deep and long-lasting, and stock market rallies usually prove themselves to be illusory. In one study, Carmen Reinhart of the University of Maryland and Kenneth Rogoff of Harvard studied the impact of financial crises on the housing and stock markets in a wide variety of countries. Their conclusions were sobering. On average, the peak-to-trough decline for stocks in the aftermath of financial crises was 55 per cent and lasted three and a half years. For housing, the average decline from the peak was 35 per cent with the slump lasting for an average of six years. The academics also found that, in the country where the crisis occurred, government debt usually soared in the aftermath. The reason was not the impact of major stimulus packages; rather, it was the result of a dramatic decline in government revenues as businesses suffered and citizens lost their jobs.[12]

STAY CLOSE TO SHORE

In November 2008, Circuit City Stores Inc. became the largest U.S. retailer thus far to file for bankruptcy protection. The filing leaves creditors on the hook for some $625 million they are owed, and throws forty thousand employees in the U.S. out of work.[13] The chain reaction of clogged credit markets, plunging consumer confidence and sluggish global growth will affect the world economy until at least the middle of 2010—although others think this slowdown could go on for much longer. In January 2009 *The Times* quoted Robert Shiller, the famed economics professor at Yale University who correctly predicted the

Internet bubble in 2000, as saying, "We could be facing a decade of real weakness."[14] Clearly, this is not the time for investors to pin their life savings on the hopes of a quick turnaround.

But if you are looking for a little action while you wait for the turnaround to finally happen, one place to park your dough is at the movies—a sector often resilient to economic uncertainty, as it proved itself during the 1930s. The *Globe and Mail* reported that Cineplex Galaxy Income Fund (Cineplex Galaxy being Canada's largest movie chain) saw ticket sales of 63.5 million during 2008, with 25 per cent of those occurring during the last three months of the year when the economy and the consumer were in the tank.[15] Movie house stocks tend to do quite well when times are tough. Not only is a night at the movies a cheap form of escapism, but you can see how things are doing with your investment while you're at it.

Electric utilities and pipelines are another good way to stay safe while scooping some cash in the form of a dividend. Pipeline companies such as TransCanada PipeLines Ltd., a company headquartered in Calgary that operates more than fifty-nine thousand kilometres of natural gas pipeline, are a defensive way to stay put.[16] On the electric utility side, a company such as Emera Inc., the principal supplier of electricity to Nova Scotians, is another way to ride out the storm. Cash flows for regulated utilities are pretty well bulletproof, since they are set by provincial or federal regulators. In essence, these businesses are monopolies that aren't overly dependent on the state of the national or global economy and they aren't affected by what is happening in the world of commodities, either. Better yet, you're paid to wait with average dividend yields of approximately 4 per cent for the Canadian pipeline and utility universe.

One company that is supersizing itself during the economic slowdown is McDonald's Corporation. The hamburger chain has seen traffic at its stores increase, as people who still want to eat out trade down to cheaper fare. As a result, the company is looking at adding more than a thousand stores globally over the next few years. Several new menu items have been a hit with the consumer, such as a $7.95 "all you can eat" bottomless lunch of salads, soup and garlic bread added in September 2008.[17] Another hit has been their coffee and muffin combo, priced right at just $1.29.[18]

In a recession, consumers sit on their wallets. And when they do buy something it's generally the cheaper alternative. Retailers who stock too much inventory or, worse yet, the expensive kind that falls out of favour when times are tough can be in for a rude awakening. The *Financial Times* reported the chief executive of Saks, a luxury department store in the U.S., saying in November 2008, "I don't think any of us anticipated the high-end customers were going to fall off as dramatically as they have."[19]

Supermarkets and drug stores are generally considered good defensive areas of the market for investors sitting on the sidelines until the economy turns. Both the food retailers, such as Metro Inc., and the drug stores, such as Shoppers Drug Mart or Jean Coutu Pharmacy, turn their inventory over very quickly. Unlike the U.S. where a myriad of drug coverage plans has hurt earnings, Canadian pharmacies are generally profitable.

BOND BLUES

Over the last twenty years or so, bond investors have had it pretty good, with high returns and low risk as interest rates have steadily marched lower. In a survey conducted for the *Financial Times*, institutional fund managers predicted that, for 2009, high-grade corporate bonds would outperform other asset classes.[20] They may be right for 2009, but there's no reason to expect that bonds will perform like champs in 2010 and beyond.

Mention bonds and you tend to draw a blank stare; most people are more familiar with stocks. In bond investing, you're lending money to a corporation or a government for a fixed period of time. They pay you a rate of interest, or coupon, for your trouble and promise to pay you back on a certain date. While you're waiting to get your principal back, bond prices move up and down in response to market conditions. When times are good, stocks are generally the way to go, but when times are bad and central banks are slashing interest rates in the hope of getting the economy going again, bonds are usually the safer bet.[21]

With interest rates already at rock bottom levels, how much further can they drop? Without the major tailwind of falling interest rates, the success that bond investors have had over the last few decades is unlikely to be repeated. If you are going to buy bonds, particularly corporate bonds, however, then I would recommend buying a bond ETF, such as the various iShares products, which include the iShares Canadian Corporate Bond Index Fund. ETFs, or bond mutual funds, offer you broad diversification without the concentration risk of a blow-up in a single bond.

WHIPLASH

Behind the economic and stock market mayhem, a more fundamental shift is occurring—one that will ultimately benefit Canada. Unless you believe that we're going back to the Smoot-Hawley world of the early 1930s, then you know it's only a matter of time until the world begins to grow again. Globalization has flattened the world and given hundreds of millions of people in developing countries a chance at what we already take for granted: a better life.

The path forward won't be uniform, and it won't be equal. But global growth *will* happen, if for no other reason than there are so many people in the developing world. A remarkable, and telling, event occurred in Washington, D.C., on November 15, 2008: the first G20 summit. The meeting involved leaders of the richest twenty countries in the world, collectively representing 90 per cent of global GDP. Prior to this, it had always been the G7 or the G8 that met annually—the rest were simply excluded.*

---

*The Group of Seven, or G7, includes the finance ministers of the seven largest industrialized countries in the world: Canada, France, Germany, Italy, Japan, the United Kingdom and the United States. The G8 also includes Russia.

But now the world has changed. Twenty years of living on borrowed money has finally caught up with the U.S., and the solution to its problems will involve China and America's other bankers. As a result, capital and opportunity will inevitably start to flow east. Those who understand the forces that are shaping and transforming our world will be huge beneficiaries of what is a once-in-a-lifetime garage sale going on in the share prices of corporate Canada. Asia is rising and Canada is rising right along with it. America will always matter, but the economic reality is that Asia will matter more.

This book is about change and how to profit from it. The future is unfolding right now. Louis Pasteur, the French chemist whose work gave us pasteurization, once famously remarked, "Chance favours the prepared mind." Here's to making the most of our chances!

CHAPTER SUMMARY

- The global financial crisis will go on for far longer than experts have predicted.
- A fundamental reordering of the global economy is already well underway.
- Increasingly, Asia will be the centre of the global economy.
- Protectionism is a threat to the prosperity that globalization has built over the last three decades.
- Corporate bonds will be a good bet, but only in the short term.
- Cash, utilities and consumer staples will be good sectors in which to park your money until the global economy begins to move forward.
- Canada's star is rising and will soon get the global recognition and investment it deserves.

NOTES

CHAPTER 2

1. Kevin Connor, "The Subprime Motive: Billions in Revenues and Bonuses," *subPrimer*, http://subprimer.org/node/9.

CHAPTER 3

1. *The Economist*, "Sittin' on the Dock of a Bay," November 22, 2008, 52.
2. AFP, "World Economic Situation 'Grim,' Says China's Hu," November 22, 2008.
3. Hoover's, http://www.hoovers.com/.
4. Tanya Palta, "Six Facts About Bollywood," Our Bollywood, September 26, 2006, http://www.ourbollywood.com/2006/09/six_facts_about_bollywood.html.
5. Na Liu, email message to author, December 8, 2008.
6. Stephen Roach, "Uncomfortable Truths About Our World After the Bubble," *Financial Times*, December 3, 2008.
7. Na Liu, "Equity Research," Scotia Capital, December 9, 2008.
8. Intel, http://www.intel.com/.
9. *The Economist*, "Dr Keynes's Chinese Patient," November 15, 2008, 16.

CHAPTER 4

1. Kathy M. Kristof and Andrea Chang, "IndyMac Bank Seized by Federal Regulators," *Los Angeles Times*, July 12, 2008.

2. Siobhan Kennedy and Dearbail Jordan, "RBS Emerges Victorious in Fight for ABN Amro," *Times Online* (London), October 8, 2007, http://business.timesonline.co.uk/tol/business/industry_sectors/banking_and_finance/article2613228.ece.

3. Ben St-Pierre, email message to author, December 5, 2008.

4. Shawn Tully, "Wall Street's Money Machine Breaks Down," *Fortune*, November 12, 2007.

5. David Gaffen, "Merrill's CDO Pioneer," *Wall Street Journal*, October 25, 2007.

6. See note 4 above.

7. Gregory Cresci, "Merrill, Citigroup Record CDO Fees Earned in Top Growth Market," Bloomberg, August 30, 2005.

8. Ibid.

9. Miles Weiss, "Merrill Lynch's O'Neil Departs With $161.5 Million," Bloomberg, October 30, 2007.

10. U.S. Federal Reserve, "Federal Reserve Release," press release, September 11, 2001.

11. Caroline Baum, "Jim Bunning's Capitalism Pitch Is Strike Zone," Bloomberg, July 18, 2008.

12. David Oakley and Michael Mackenzie, "Concerns Mount on Ability to Fund State Debt," *Financial Times*, November 30, 2008.

13. Julia Werdigier, "U.K. Bank Rescue Plan, a Model for Others, Is in Trouble," *International Herald Tribune*, December 14, 2008.

14. Edmund Clarke (president and chief executive officer, TD Bank Financial Group), keynote speech, INSEAD Alumni Dinner, Toronto, October 28, 2008.

15. Paul Vieira, "Our Financial System Sparks Interest: Carney," *Financial Post*, November 10, 2008.

16. John Gray, "Canada's Top 50 Brands," *Canadian Business*, June 18, 2007.
17. Neha Singh, "Credit Card Industry May Cut $2 Trillion of Lines: Analyst," *New York Times,* December 1, 2008.
18. Philip Preville, "The Good News About the Bad Times," *Toronto Life*, February 2009, http://www.torontolife.com/features/good-news-about-bad-times/?pageno=1.

CHAPTER 5

1. U.S. Federal Reserve, "Federal Open Market Committee Statement," press release, December 16, 2008.
2. Christopher Rugaber, "Federal Deficit on Pace to Reach Record $1T," *BusinessWeek*, December 10, 2008.
3. Ben Bernanke, "Deflation: Making Sure 'It' Doesn't Happen Here" (remarks of Governor Ben S. Bernanke before the National Economists Club, Washington D.C., November 21, 2002).
4. Brook Larmer, "The Real Price of Gold," *National Geographic*, January 2009.
5. Ibid.
6. Vahid Fathi, "Our Updated Take on Gold Prices," *Morningstar.com*, December 15, 2008.
7. Trevor Turnbull, email message to author, December 22, 2008.

CHAPTER 6

1. Derek Holt, Karen Cordes, and Mary Webb, "Canada's Mortgage Market Is NOT Like the U.S.," *Capital Points*, Global Economic Research, Scotiabank Group, September 26, 2008.
2. Tavia Grant, "Loonie Poised to Rise: Goldman," *Globe and Mail*, December 18, 2008.
3. Jacquie McNish and Greg McArthur, "How High-Risk Mortgages Crept North," *Globe and Mail*, December 13, 2008.

4. CMHC, "CMHC Enhances Flexibility and Reduces Monthly Mortgage Costs," press release, June 26, 2006.

5. Genworth Financial Canada, "Genworth Financial Canada Making Homeownership More Affordable for Canadians with 40-year Amortization," press release, October 10, 2006.

6. Drew Hasselback, "CMHC Adds 40-Year Term, 100% Funds as Products," *Financial Post*, November 18, 2006.

7. "David Dodge Criticizes CMHC for 'Unhelpful' Actions," *CBC News*, October 30, 2006.

8. Department of Finance (Canada), "Government of Canada Moves to Protect, Strengthen Canadian Housing Market," press release, July 9, 2008.

9. Julian Beltrame, "Bank of Canada Sounds Debt Alarm," The Canadian Press, December 11, 2008.

10. See note 1 above.

11. Janet Morrisey, "Option ARM Resets Could Deepen Housing Turmoil," *Investment News*, September 15, 2008.

12. Mara Der Hovanesian, "Nightmare Mortgages," *BusinessWeek*, September 11, 2006.

13. Paul Waldie, "Homeowners Left to 'Hope and Pray' as Foreclosures Soar," *Globe and Mail*, October 1, 2008.

14. Benjamin Tal, "Canadian Cities: An Economic Snapshot," *Metro Monitor, Economics & Strategy*, CIBC World Markets, December 17, 2008.

15. "Federal and Provincial Tax Rates, Brackets and Surtaxes–2007," KPMG.

16. Lori McLeod, "Housing Sales Hit 20-Year Low as Real Estate Slump Widens," *Globe and Mail*, December 16, 2008.

17. Data from CMHC, JSI Inc. estimates.

18. Christopher Donville, "Housing Slump Hits Canada as Seller Offers C$100,000 Deal Bonus," *Bloomberg News*, November 19, 2008.

19. See note 14 above.

20. Konrad Yakabuski, Virgini Galt and Greg Scott Norval, "The Gloom Spreads North," *Globe and Mail*, October 4, 2008.

21. "World Economic Outlook, Housing and the Business Cycle," International Monetary Fund, World Economic and Financial Surveys, April 2008, 113.

22. Based on data from CMHC and JSI Inc. estimates.

23. Amy Williamson (real estate agent, Bosley Real Estate Ltd.), in discussion with the author, December 17, 2008.

24. Nick Boothby, "Get the Best (ROI) Return on Investment with Your Renos and Upgrades," Royal LePage, http://www.inthebeach.com/reno_roi.html.

25. Garry Marr, "Canadians Pushed Back Into Rentals," *National Post*, December 12, 2008.

26. Amy Goldbloom, "Housing Market Froth Finally Evaporating," RBC, May 2008.

27. Virginia Galt, "Condo Building Boom Screeches to a Halt," *Globe and Mail*, December 9, 2008.

28. William Tharp (senior economist, Dundee Securities), in discussion with the author, December 16, 2008.

CHAPTER 7

1. *The Economist*, "The Cracks Are Showing," June 28, 2008, 36.

2. Ibid.

3. "Quebec Calls Inquiry Into Deadly Overpass Collapse," *CBC News*, October 1, 2006.

4. "9 Thought Dead as Minneapolis Bridge Collapses," *MSNBC.com*, (August 2, 2007), http://www.msnbc.msn.com/id/20079534/.

5. "Renewing America's Infrastructure, a Citizen's Guide," American Society of Civil Engineers, 2001.

6. "United States Infrastructure Report Q4 2008," Business Monitor International Ltd., October 2008, 6.

7. Ibid.

8. Jeffrey Rubin, Avery Shenfeld, Benjamin Tal, Peter Buchanan, Warren Lovely and David Bezic, "Infrastructure: The New Frontier," *Occasional Report #60*, Economics & Strategy, CIBC World Markets, March 26, 2007.

9. See note 1 above.

10. Tim Reid, "Barack Obama Reveals Stimulus Package That Could Exceed $1 Trillion," *Times Online* (London), December 8, 2008, http://www.timesonline.co.uk/tol/news/world/us_and_americas/ us_elections/article5303652.ece.

11. Benjamin Tal, "Capitalizing on the Upcoming Infrastructure Stimulus," *Occasional Report #66*, CIBC World Markets, January 26, 2009.

12. See note 8 above.

13. "Build & Rebuild," *Thematic Investing Focus*, Citigroup Global Markets, April 11, 2008.

14. See note 8 above.

15. Rina Chandran, "Indian Wealth Brings High Road Toll," *Toronto Star*, August 30, 2008.

16. John Baird, letter to the editor, *National Post*, December 20, 2008.

17. Benjamin Tal, "No Cracks in Canadian Infrastructure Stocks," CIBC World Markets Inc., December 19, 2007.

18. See note 16 above.

19. Government of Alberta, "2008-11 Capital Plan Delivers $22.2 Billion for Municipalities, Housing, Hospitals, Schools, and Roads," press release, April 22, 2008.

20. Peter Reina and Gary J. Tulacz, "The Top 200 International Design Firms," ENR, July 21, 2008.

21. Bombardier, http://www.bombardier.com/.

22. Bertrand Marotte, "Bombardier Rides Rails to Profit Increase," *Globe and Mail*, December 15, 2008.

23. Helga Loverseed, "Montreal Not Content to Contain Itself," *Globe and Mail*, December 9, 2008.

24. Konrad Yakabuski, "New England Lusts for Quebec's Power," *Globe and Mail*, December 30, 2008.

25. John Spence, "ETFs for Infrastructure: Obama's Plan for U.S. Spending Could Help Construction Stocks, Other Sectors," *Marketwatch.com*, January 5, 2009, http://www.marketwatch.com/news/story/infrastructure-etfs-may-benefit-obamas/story.aspx?guid=%7BDD48356E%2DD1AC%2D40AE%2D8BC2%2D11 17358DFFBD%7D&dist=msr_7.

26. See note 11 above.

CHAPTER 8

1. Andrew Garthwaite, Mary Curtis, Angello Chan, Eric Lopez, John McNulty, Charlie Mills, Julian Mitchell, Nicole Parent, Richard Kersley and Gary Balter, "Water," *The New Perspective Series*, Credit Suisse, June 7, 2007.

2. Benjamin Tal, *"Tapping Into Water,"* CIBC World Markets, November 7, 2006.

3. Erin Anderssen, "Maude Barlow: The Al Gore of H$_2$O," *Globe and Mail*, October 25, 2008.

4. *The Economist*, "Running Dry," August 23, 2008, 53.

5. *The Economist*, "A Shortage of Capital Flows," October 11, 2008, 61.

6. See note 1 above.

7. Martin Roberts, "Spain Can See Bottom," *National Post*, May 15, 2008.

8. See note 2 above.

9. See note 1 above.

10. See note 4 above.

11. See note 1 above.

12. Editorial, *Toronto Star*, August 5, 2008.

13. "Federal Water Policy," Environment Canada, 1987.

14. Justin Sussman, email message to author, May 7, 2009.
15. Marcel Boyer, "Freshwater Exports for the Development of Quebec's Blue Gold" (research paper, Montreal Economic Institute, August 2008).
16. See note 2 above.
17. See note 1 above.

CHAPTER 9

1. Paul Cashin and John McDermott, "The Long-Run Behavior of Commodity Prices: Small Trends and Big Variability" (working paper, International Monetary Fund, IMF Working Paper WP/01/68).
2. Gary Gorton and Geert K. Rouwenhorst, "Facts and Fantasies About Commodity Futures" (working paper, Yale International Center for Finance, Paper No. 04-20, June 14, 2004).
3. See note 1 above.
4. Martin Garzaron, "The Investment Case for Natural Resources," City of London Investment Management Company Limited, March 2007.
5. Rita Raagas De Ramos, "Fund Managers Make the Case for Asia," *Asian Investor*, January 6, 2009, http://www.asianinvestor.net/print. aspx?CIID=132205.
6. See note 2 above.

CHAPTER 10

1. "Did Speculation Fuel Oil Price Swings?" *60 Minutes*, January 11, 2009.
2. David Corn, "Foreclosure Phil," *Motherjones.com*, May 28, 2008, http://www.motherjones.com/politics/2008/05/foreclosure-phil.
3. Eric Lipton, "Gramm and the Enron Loophole," *New York Times*, November 17, 2008.
4. David Barboza, "UBS Closing Trading Floor It Acquired From Enron," *New York Times*, November 21, 2002.

5. See note 1 above.

6. See note 4 above.

7. Dawn Kopecki and Shannon D. Harrington, "Fannie, Freddie Tumble on Solvency Concerns, UBS Price Cut," *Bloomberg News*, July 10, 2008.

8. Daniel Whitten, "Senators Offer Bills Curbing Commodities Speculation," *Bloomberg News*, July 11, 2008.

9. "Stocks Tumble on Treasury Plan Uncertainty," *Briefing.com*, September 22, 2008, http://www.briefing.com/GeneralContent/ Investor/Active/ArticlePopup/ArticlePopup.aspx?ArticleId=SI20 080922161800.

10. "Indonesia to Withdraw from OPEC," *BBC*, May 28, 2008, http:// news.bbc.co.uk/2/hi/business/7423008.stm.

11. International Energy Agency, "World Energy Outlook 2008" (presentation to the press, November 12, 2008).

12. Shawn McCarthy, "The Cost of the Next Barrel," *Globe and Mail*, June 14, 2008.

13. See note 11 above.

14. Ibid.

15. Heather Scoffield, "Economy: Energy Windfall," *Globe and Mail*, June 21, 2008.

16. Eric Reguly, "Shifting Sands: How Alberta's Oil Boom Has Changed Canada Forever: The Bottom Line," *Globe and Mail*, February 2, 2008.

17. *Financial Post Business Magazine*, "A Global Contender, Massive Unconventional Petroleum Resources Are Making Canada a Heavyweight Challenger in the Energy World," October 7, 2008.

18. Erin Anderssen, Shawn McCarthy and Eric Reguly, "Shifting Sands: How Alberta's Oil Boom Has Changed Canada Forever: Part 1," *Globe and Mail*, January 23, 2008.

19. See note 17 above.

20. Eric Reguly, "It's a Dud, But It's All Ours: Protected Companies Always Hurt Shareholders in Some Way—Just Look at Petro-Canada," *Globe and Mail*, October 31, 2008.

CHAPTER 11

1. *The Economist*, "Ore-Some," February 20, 2008.
2. Eric Reguly and Eric Hoffman, "Boom Will Return, Don't Ask When," *Globe and Mail*, October 25, 2008.
3. Andy Hoffman, "Closed Mines, Broken Dreams in the Town That Nickel Built," *Globe and Mail*, December 5, 2008.
4. "The Collapse in Copper Consumption: How Long? How Deep? Will the Copper Industry Be Ready for the Recovery?" Bloomsbury Minerals Economics Ltd., January 13, 2009.
5. Greg Keenan, "China Outruns the U.S. in Vehicle Sales," *Globe and Mail*, February 4, 2009.
6. *The Economist*, "A Global Love Affair," November 13, 2008.
7. *The Economist*, "Opportunity Knocks—As Long As the Protectionists Don't Spoil It," September 18, 2008.
8. "2009 Uranium Market Outlook," Ux Consulting Company LLC, January 13, 2009.
9. Eric Reguly, "The Oligarch Shuffle," *Globe and Mail*, February 7, 2009.
10. Andy Hoffman, "Axed Xstrata Bid Signals Metals in for Leaner Times," *Globe and Mail*, October 2, 2009.
11. Teck Cominco, http://www.teckcominco.com/.
12. HudBay Minerals Inc., "RBC Capital Markets Global Mining and Minerals" (company presentation, June 10, 2008).
13. First Quantum Minerals, http://www.first-quantum.com/.
14. Horizons BetaPro ETFs, http://www.hbpetfs.com/.

CHAPTER 12

1. Stewart Sinclair and Paul Waldie, "Feeding Frenzy," *Globe and Mail*, May 31, 2008.

2. Minority Staff of the Permanent Subcommittee on Investigations of the Committee on Governmental Affairs, United States Senate, "U.S. Strategic Petroleum Reserve: Recent Policy Has Increased Costs to Consumers But Not Overall U.S. Energy Security" (report, U.S. Government Printing Office, Washington, 2003).

3. See note 1 above.

4. Minutes of UN-backed forum in Iceland on sustainable development.

5. "The State of Food Insecurity in the World 2008," Food and Agricultural Organization (FAO) of the United Nations, 2008.

6. *The Economist*, "The New Face of Hunger," April 19, 2008, 33.

7. Randy Schnepf, "Energy Use in Agriculture: Background and Issues," Congressional Research Service, The Library of Congress, November 19, 2004.

8. Danielle Nierenberg, "Meat Production and Consumption Grow," Worldwatch Institute, http://www.worldwatch.org/brain/media/pdf/pubs/vs/2003_meat.pdf.

9. Christopher L. Delgado, "Animal Source Foods to Improve Micronutrient Nutrition and Human Function in Developing Countries," *Journal of Nutrition* 133 (2003): 3907S–3910S.

10. Hans Schreier, "Water and Agriculture: Harvesting Water Before Harvesting the Crop," http://www.sfu.ca/cstudies/science/resources/water/pdf/Water-Ch17.pdf.

11. "Cornell Ecologist's Study Finds that Producing Ethanol and Biodiesel from Corn and Other Crops Is Not Worth the Energy," Cornell University News Service, July 5, 2005.

12. See note 5 above.

13. Amit Sharma, email message to author, February 3, 2009.

14. *The Economist*, "A Harvest of Disgrace," May 22, 2008.

15. Mark Connelly, Nils-Bertil Wallin, Jinsong Du, Semyon Mironov, Nurlan Zhakupov, Luiz Otavio Campos, Robert Moskow, Rhian

Tucker, Mohamad Hawa, Mohsin Mangi, Rohan Gallagher, Lars Kjellberg and Sidney Yeh, "How Farm Commercialization Will Drive the Next Decade of Growth," Credit Suisse, September 3, 2008.

16. Tony A. A. Heaps, "Potash Politics—Canadian O.P.E.C." The Organization of Potash Exporting Companies, *Corporate Knights*, Issue 26, Winter 2009, 19.

17. *The Economist*, "The Next Green Revolution—Europe May Not Like It, But Genetic Modification Is Transforming Agriculture," February 21, 2008.

18. Richard Black, "GM Seeds Can 'Last for 10 Years'" *BBC News*, April 2, 2008, http://news.bbc.co.uk/2/hi/science/nature/7324654.stm.

19. Eric Reguly, "Soaring Food Costs Sow Doubts Over Europe's GM Policy," *Globe and Mail*, June 25, 2008.

CHAPTER 13

1. Keith Bachman, "Research In Motion Initiating Coverage Report," BMO Capital Markets, October 28, 2008.

2. Duff MacDonald, "The BlackBerry Brain Trust," *Wired.com*, January 2005, http://www.wired.com/wired/archive/13.01/perimeter.html.

3. Perimeter Institute for Theoretical Physics, http://www.perimeterinstitute.ca/news/.

4. University of Waterloo Co-operative Education & Career Services, http://www.cecs.uwaterloo.ca/about/.

5. University of Waterloo Faculty of Mathematics, http://www.math.uwaterloo.ca/.

6. Douglas Wright (former president of the University of Waterloo), in discussion with the author, January 1, 2009.

7. "Bill Gates Draws a Crowd at Waterloo University," *CTV.ca*, October 14, 2005, http://www.ctv.ca.

8. Gordon Pitts, "Lessons from Kitchener-Waterloo," *Globe and Mail*, April 24, 2006.

9. Open Text Corporation, http://www.opentext.com/.

10. David George-Cosh, "Waterloo Targets Gifted with Innovative Dorm," *Financial Post*, September 9, 2008.

11. See note 8 above.

12. "Two New Research Centres Open at Guelph," *eSource Canada Business News Network*, October 20, 2008.

13. Megan Ogilvie, "The Future of Food? U of G's 'Enviropig' Brings Genetically Engineered Meal Closer to the Table," *Guelph Mercury*, December 2, 2008.

14. Brett Bundale, "Canadians Aim to Grow First Plant on Moon," *Montreal Gazette*, July 16, 2008.

15. "Bell-Northern Research," *Wikipedia*, http://en.wikipedia.org/wiki/Bell-Northern_Research.

16. Gordon Pitts, "Canadian Innovation," *Globe and Mail*, January 17, 2009.

17. Thomson Reuters, http://www.thomsonreuters.com/about/.

18. Vince Valentini and Eli Papakirykos, "Thomson Reuters Corp.," TD Newcrest, April 17, 2008.

19. Bombardier, http://www.bombardier.com/en.corporate/investor-relations/.

20. Jay Boehmer, "Wal-Mart Wields Corp. Fleet," *Business Travel News*, June 5, 2006.

21. Bombardier, "A Family of Aircraft With Exceptional Value" (presentation, November 2008), http://www.bombardier.com/files/en/supporting_docs/20081111_Research_Capital_Gary_Scott_CSeries_Final.pdf.

22. Richard Tse, Hubert Mak and Manik Verma, "MacDonald, Dettwiler and Associates," National Bank Financial, April 13, 2009.

23. David Newman, email message to author, May 5, 2009.

24. Richard Florida, "The Creative City," *Toronto Life*, 2008, 38.

25. Richard Florida and James Milway, "Creative Class the Most Recession-Proof," *Globe and Mail*, November 24, 2008.

26. Roger L. Martin and Richard Florida, "Ontario in the Creative Age," Martin Prosperity Institute, February 2009.

27. David Psutka, "Room for Improvement in Ontario Schools: Report," *Globe and Mail*, May 22, 2008.

28. "Growing Unequal?: Income Distribution and Poverty in OECD Countries, Country Note: Canada," OECD, 2008.

29. John Henderson, email message to author, February 16, 2009.

30. "Canada: Internet Usage, Broadband and Telecommunications Reports," *Internet World Stats*, http://www.Internetworldstats.com/am/ca.htm.

CHAPTER 14

1. Rhéal Séguin, "Consumers' Outlook Grim, Poll Finds," *Globe and Mail*, January 14, 2009.

2. Bobby White and Stu Woo, "California to Delay $4 Billion in Payments," *Wall Street Journal*, January 31, 2009.

3. David Segal, "Wall Street Becomes the Target of Scorn," *International Herald Tribune*, February 2, 2009.

4. Julie Creswell and Louise Story, "Thain Exits Bank of America Amid Losses," *International Herald Tribune*, January 23, 2009.

5. Jim Kunhenn, "Top Bankers Vow to Win Back Trust," *Globe and Mail*, February 11, 2009.

6. *The Economist*, "Fixing Finance," January 22, 2009.

7. *The Economist*, "Not-so-Nice Land," January 26, 2009.

8. Marcus Gee and Brian Milner, "U.S. Must Resist Instinct to Circle the Wagons," *Globe and Mail*, February 2, 2009.

9. Marina Jiménez, "Struggling Spain Highlights Euro Zone's Plight," *Globe and Mail*, January 30, 2009.

10. Eric Reguly, "Europe's Winter of Discontent," *Globe and Mail*, February 3, 2009.

11. Randall Mikkelsen, "World Economic Crisis Is Top Security Threat: U.S.," *Reuters*, February 12, 2009.

12. Carmen M. Reinhart and Kenneth S. Rogoff, "The Aftermath of Financial Crises," School of Public Policy and Department of Economics, University of Maryland, December 19, 2008.

13. Kathryn Tam, "The Ripple Effect," *Globe and Mail*, February 6, 2009.

14. Suzy Jagger, "Leading Economist Fears Decade of Weakness in US," *Times* (London), January 12, 2009.

15. Grant Robertson, "Recession Doesn't Wound Silver Screen," *Globe and Mail*, February 13, 2009.

16. TransCanada PipeLines, http://www.transcanada.com/company/index.html.

17. Marina Strauss, "As Times Get Tough, Golden Arches Shine," *Globe and Mail*, October 23, 2008.

18. Grant Robertson, "Hungry Times, and McDonald's Is Lovin' It," *Globe and Mail*, January 27, 2009.

19. "High-End Brands Find Credit Crisis Is Hard to Wear," *Financial Times*, November 28, 2008.

20. Esther Bintliff, "Asset Managers Turn to Corporate Bonds," *Financial Times*, January 5, 2009.

21. Dianne Maley, "Shelter From the Storm," *Globe and Mail*, January 28, 2009.

INDEX